THE
MIND
AT
PEACE

BASED ON A TRUE STORY

BY

Jeffrey Zavik

Peppertree Press
Sarasota, Florida

For information regarding permission,
call 941-922-2662 or contact us at our website:
www.peppertreepublishing.com or write to:
the Peppertree Press, LLC.
Attention: Publisher
1269 First Street, Suite 7
Sarasota, Florida 34236

ISBN: 978-1-936051-44-1

Library of Congress Number: 2009932592

Printed in the U.S.A.

Printed August 2009

An Invitation From The Author

You are reading this book for a reason – perhaps not the one you think. Our world is at a unique point in time where life is moving at lightning speed, stressful events are at all time highs and the future health and well being of our entire planet creates a shadow of uncertainty onto every plan for the future we make. I invite you, just for the moment to be open to the possibility of a way out of all of this. Let me explain…

Bad news surrounds us everywhere we turn. Yet in spite of what many predict is a very bleak and uncertain future, nature itself provides the antidote. Where poison ivy is found growing, one often finds jewelweed (a proven natural remedy for those exposed to poison ivy) nearby.

I invite you to read this novel with the possibility that what Jennifer Albright, a kindergarten teacher discovers - the remedy each and every one of us has available is very nearby; in fact, within our own hearts and minds. As you discover the best ways for you to set your own mind at peace, I'm confident you'll see how far reaching it can be and how our world could in fact be, a better place. It is my hope that this story helps you to discover the peace that lays within you.

To my wonderful wife, Cher.
Thank you for making this possible!

Chapter 1

It was just another Monday morning in kinder-garten. With her back to the class, the teacher, Jenni-fer Albright stood writing the date on the blackboard. Behind her, she could hear the happy laughter of her five- and six-year-old students, some of them still putting away their backpacks and lunchboxes in the row of cubbies near the door, others rushing between the classroom tables, thrilled to see each other again after the weekend. Suddenly, she picked out from the welter of excited voices two sentences that froze her in place: "Are you here for show and tell?" and "Is that gun real?"

Jennifer's throat went dry and her jaw clenched. Feeling as if the air around her had thickened and curled around her limbs, she turned slowly and deliberately. Silhouetted in the classroom door was a man she had never seen before. He was obviously homeless, dressed in an Army surplus jacket and shapeless, torn jeans. His matted grey hair and beard made his age impossible to guess, and his small, dark eyes were almost hidden by his heavy brow. He held a small pistol loosely in his right hand.

Jennifer appraised her situation wordlessly. Half of the class had not even noticed the man. They were still engaged in the sort of playing, running around, fidgeting and fighting that started all of their mornings at school. The other half of the class had formed a rough semicircle around the man, absorbed by his unlikely attire—the middle-class town of Greenfield attracted few, if any, homeless people—and transfixed by the gun in his hand.

Rooted to the spot and still holding her chalk in her hand, as if the man was an apparition who might vanish as quickly as he had come, Jennifer stared helplessly. The man shambled in a meandering path into the classroom and stood in the middle of the story time carpet, rocking almost imperceptibly on the balls of his feet. His eyes darted around the classroom. For a moment, they settled on the brightly colored alphabet on the bulletin board. Jennifer felt a cold terror travel up from the base of her spine as the man's eyes shifted again and fell on the tops of two of the children's heads, who had followed him from the doorway. The two children, Wendell and Anna, were gazing up at him, their faces filled with eager curiosity. He seemed to barely notice them before his focus shifted again.

He's mentally ill, Jennifer realized, still following his every distracted movement.

Immediately after this, she thought, And he has a gun, the words forming and reforming in her mind, blinking like a headline on the Times Square news ticker.

He...has...a...gun.

In an instant, something within Jennifer shifted, and she went from abject terror and a mind chattering with thought and fear to a state of almost impossible relaxation, one that she had seldom experienced in her life and therefore one that she did not completely trust. She tried to understand where her mind was taking her. Was it to a place of calm control, so that she could handle this unexpected, terrifying situation with dignity, diplomacy, and grace? Or was it to a place of surrender, a kind of giving in to the horrible tragedy that was about to ensue, one that she was powerless to prevent?

Jennifer, an organized, meticulous, attractive twenty-nine-year-old woman, had always prided herself on her ability to think her way out of any difficult situation, at work, with her family, or in her (currently non-existent) social life. But now, she struggled against some barrier that had sprung up uninvited in her mind. To her immense frustration she found that she could not think at all. Every fiber of her being was ordering her to formulate a plan, to use brain power to conquer the situation. But not a single thought was coalescing in her head other than the simple, basic, undeniable words that continued to flash on and off with neon clarity: He...has...a...gun.

By now the entire class had noticed the intruder's presence, and divided their attention between him and their teacher, as their little minds tried to gage how to react. Maybe he was there for show and tell. Or maybe he was a bad, dangerous man, and something frightening was going to happen.

For a long moment, every child in the class looked imploringly at Jennifer, waiting for her to take the lead, to interpret the situation, to take control.

And yet Jennifer remained rooted to her spot by the blackboard, willing thought to direct her, but thought would not come.

In that instant, frustrated that her mental apparatus, which had carried her from success to success in her years at school, and which had allowed her to develop a successful career as a kindergarten teacher—the only job she had ever really wanted—had failed her, Jennifer gave up on the conscious need to think. Instead, she studied the man, who studied her, gun in hand, finger on the trigger, surrounded by children, a few of whom had begun to cry.

The crying snapped Jennifer out of her dazed state. She was immediately flooded by a sense of relief, of accepting the quiet state of her mind.

"Show and tell," she heard herself say out loud. "Class, we're going to begin today with show and tell. Please make a circle."

Observing herself as if from a distance, Jennifer wondered where those words had come from. She felt as though she wasn't forming them herself, but was instead speaking words that had been generated somewhere deep within her and that she had repeated as if taking dictation from that previously untapped source. Was it God? Was it her subconscious? She neither knew nor cared. All she knew was that she had to trust that voice, because it was the only thing she possessed that could possibly equalize the situation with the gunman. One false move and…she stopped the half-thought in its tracks, somehow aware that it could only transmit fear through her eyes and demeanor to the children and then to the stranger, likely triggering horrific results.

Her command to form a circle for show and tell still hung in the air, and the children, uniformly curious about their visitor, some afraid, some not, obediently formed a circle around the man. Jennifer, acting again without thought, carried a chair from behind her desk to the center of the circle where the man stood, and gently indicated with a calm gesture that the man should be seated.

He locked eyes with Jennifer, and she could tell that she was looking into the eyes of a mentally unstable individual. His haggard face and the acrid smell that seeped from his sack-like clothing advertised unmistakably that he had been sleeping outside for days or longer.

Eventually, calmed by her thoughtful yet persistent gaze, and to some extent warmed by the gesture of hospitality, he sat down.

He held the gun in his right hand as before, thumb on the safety, index finger on the trigger.

Jennifer knew nothing of guns, and in fact had never even seen a real one outside of an occasional movie one date or another had brought her to. She had nothing against guns but had given them very little thought over the course of her lifetime. It was just not part of her upbringing to own one, and its presence in the hand of this individual would have been overwhelmingly terrifying, if the apparatus with which she formed thought had not entirely shut down and been replaced by this other, less obvious source of direction.

Keeping her eyes on the drifter at all times, Jennifer walked to the corner of the classroom, where she took a stool and seated herself upon it a few feet from the stranger, as she did with any guest who came to the classroom.

The children watched anxiously, unsure of how this confrontation would end, or even what it meant. They sensed, though, that their teacher would somehow make everything all right. That, of course, was what she did every day.

"We have a guest this morning," Jennifer heard herself say in tones both friendly and authoritative. "He's a new friend we haven't met yet. Class, will you say good morning to our new friend?"

Warily but dutifully, the class said, as one, "Good morning, Mr.—" And then they paused, helplessly, their eyes turning to Jennifer, because they did not know the man's name.

"May I ask your name, sir?" Jennifer asked respectfully.

The man looked extremely surprised by the question, as if he had never expected the tableau of children in front of him and the woman beside him to address him directly. Perhaps in his mind they were props or visions or something other than human beings.

"Bob," he said quietly.

"Good morning, Bob," Jennifer said, wondering yet again what gave her the courage to speak so calmly.

"Good morning, Mr. Bob," the children said in unison, as they had been taught by Jennifer on previous occasions when guests had come to the room.

"Bob's my first name," the stranger murmured, appearing taken aback by the class's welcoming words. "My last name…"

His voice trailed off as he looked around the room. "You don't need to know my last name," he added with a tone that wasn't exactly harsh but wasn't exactly friendly, either.

"Bob," Jennifer began, "are you from Greenfield?"

Bob shook his head. Jennifer waited, but Bob gave no further indication of his origins.

"Bob is not from Greenfield," Jennifer told her students, as if Bob might have been a visiting policeman or fireman or green grocer or anything other than what he was, a homeless man with a gun, his finger, as Jennifer could not help but notice all over again, on the trigger.

"Are you visiting here in Greenfield?" Jennifer asked.

Bob's thick brows darted momentarily upward. He had apparently never thought of his life in terms of visiting one place or another. He just simply went places.

"No," he said flatly.

Jennifer nodded, maintaining her calm exterior, which was matched, to her never-ending surprise, by an equally cool calmness within.

"Do you like to visit schools?" she asked.

Bob's focus slid around the room again, falling first on the children, and then on the blackboard, the posters of zoo animals in the far corner, the American flag, Jennifer's desk and the flickering screensaver on her computer, and the stacks of toys and books neatly organized around the room. The surprise and vague bewilderment in his eyes indicated to Jennifer, if not to the students, that he had no idea where he was. Jennifer took heart from this. If his intention had been to shoot up a schoolroom, he would have known he was in one, something within her told her.

"Class," Jennifer said, now addressing the children, since further conversation with Bob seemed likely to be just as unavailing, "would you like to sing a song for our new friend?"

At the mention of the word friend, Bob sucked in a sharp breath of air. Something at the edges of his eyes seemed to soften. It dawned on Jennifer that perhaps no one had called him a friend for a long, long time.

The children looked doubtful. Bob was not the sort of person to whom they were used to singing.

"Let's sing our school welcoming song," Jennifer

said, with the firmness of a kindergarten teacher who expects to get her way.

She began the song, and raised her eyebrows at the children with an expression expecting compliance.

"This school is my school…this school is your school…" she began.

A few at a time, the children joined her, transfixed by the sight of this stranger and the extraordinary calmness with which their teacher was greeting him.

"We love to learn here, we love to play here," the children chorused.

They came to the end of the words—"This school was made for you and me," and Jennifer nodded appreciatively.

"Nicely done, class," she said. And to Bob: "Bob, did you like our song?"

Bob sat for a long time without answering. The class studied him, less in fear now and more with a sense of questioning. The children could tell, as children can, that something was wrong with him, but they were far too polite, or scared, or both, to say so.

"Yes," Bob finally said. "That's a good song."

Jennifer was about to ask him another question, when Austin, a slight blonde boy with a dusting of impish freckles, put up his hand.

"I have to go to the bathroom," Austin said matter-of-factly. Jennifer and Bob, equally surprised, studied the little boy, wondering if he had some sort of ulterior motive.

He didn't. He simply had to go to the bathroom.

Jennifer pointed toward the door, holding Austin's gaze for a deliberate moment, as if to communicate in that glance that he should tell someone, anyone, about the situation going on in the room.

A sober, business-like expression crept over Austin's face, and he gave a small, almost imperceptible nod, as if he understood her request.

Jennifer looked at Bob, asking with her eyes if it was all right for the little boy to go to the bathroom. Bob shrugged.

"He can go," Bob said.

And off Austin went.

"Children," Jennifer said, once again her mind on some sort of autopilot that she had never experienced before, "would you like to sing our new friend Bob the alphabet?"

And they did. They ended up singing Bob half a dozen songs—the alphabet, "There Was a Farmer

Who Had a Dog," "Three Blind Mice," and other songs that Jennifer had been teaching them over the course of the school year. When they got to the song about Barney, to the enormous surprise of Jennifer and the other children, Bob began to sing along. As they came to the end of the song, Bob held the last note, his gravelly voice hanging in the air just a few moments too long. He had lifted his eyes to the ceiling, and his jaw worked slightly in the silence that followed the singing.

Something in Jennifer told her to rise.

"Children," she began, "our new friend Bob has to go now. Will you please thank him for coming to visit our classroom?"

Would the gambit work? The children looked questioningly at her, because they somehow sensed that she was not responsible for Bob's introduction into the classroom. Nevertheless, they were dutiful kindergartners who loved Jennifer, and they did what she asked.

"Good-bye, Mr. Bob," they chorused.

Jolted from his reverie, Bob looked at Jennifer, thought for a long moment, and put his gun in his pocket. He stood, glanced at the children one last time, and walked out of the classroom. Through the open door Jennifer watched as two uniformed police officers intercepted the homeless man in the hallway, asked him to clasp his hands over his head, and disarmed him.

Austin had done what she'd asked.

The homeless man meekly submitted to handcuffs and was led away.

And then Jennifer, unaware that she had even breathed since the first moment she saw him standing in her classroom door, sagged to the floor. She stared wide-eyed at his retreating figure. She could feel the blood coursing through her veins and her muscles felt taught and fatigued, as if she'd just crossed the finish line of a marathon. Suddenly, her students' voices snapped her back to reality.

"Was that a real gun?" Rebecca asked.

"I didn't like him," Jose said, shaking his dark curls emphatically. "Is he coming back?"

"I hope not."

Jennifer, though she had never seen a real gun in her life, suddenly made a startling revelation.

"It was a cap gun," she said breathlessly. "It wasn't a real gun at all."

But it sure looked like one, she thought. Then, as if the floodgates of her mind were giving way at last, thoughts poured over her of what could have happened, what might have happened, what didn't happen.

She stepped quickly out of the room before her students could see her break down into sobs of relief and gratitude that they were all safe and unharmed.

She was only vaguely aware of the principal passing her, moving into her classroom as she rushed out of it. The principal's voice reached her as if from a hundred miles away, "All right, children, let's go back to our seats. Who knows what day it is?"

"I don't," Jennifer thought, collapsing against the red bricks of the hallway and, exhausted, drained, weak with relief, she slid to the floor and lost consciousness.

Chapter 2

When Jennifer came to, she found herself surrounded by paramedics and police in the principal's office. She blinked for a few times, reached for a glass of water that one of the paramedics was handing her, and looked around the room. She was lying on a couch at the back of the office, her head propped on two pillows. She noticed distractedly that her shoes were sitting neatly side by side near the arm of the couch. How had she gotten there? What was she doing there? She glanced up at the wall clock, its comforting round dial unchanged from the style she remembered when she was in elementary school twenty years earlier. Twenty minutes after nine.

"Oh, my God!" she exclaimed. "I'm late for class!"

Her words broke the considerable tension in the principal's office, and everyone laughed.

"What's so funny—" she began, but suddenly the memory of the intense ordeal she had just undergone came flooding back to her.

"Did that really happen?" she asked, searching from face to face among those present. "Are my kids okay?"

"Your kids are fine," the principal, Mack Johnson, said reassuringly. Johnson was a forty-seven-year-old former Olympic track star who had gone into education and had been the primary reason why Jennifer had come to teach at East Hills School in Greenfield. East Hills was a public school, but Johnson allowed his teachers practically free reign in terms of devising their own curricula and setting goals for their students. While most other public schools in the country "taught to the test" so as not to lose out on federal money tied to score results, East Hills managed to get sparkling test results anyway, even though each of the teachers had complete freedom to lead their classes as they saw fit. Jennifer had seen Mack Johnson on 60 Minutes when she was in high school and made up her mind even then that one day she would come to teach for him.

And now she had, and now this.

"What you did was heroic," Mack told her. Mack was a tall, lean man with a slight dusting of gray in his hair. He always wore a tweed jacket with leather-patched elbows to school, and seeing his familiar face and easy smile made Jennifer feel at home among all the uniformed officers and EMTs. "When you're feeling better," he continued, "I know the police would like to have a word with you and hear exactly what happened. After that, you can take the rest of the week off. I'll sub your class myself."

Jennifer gripped the side of the couch where she was lying down and pulled herself up to a sitting position. She blinked a few times.

"What did happen?"

"You merely saved the lives of a room full of kindergartners," Mack told her, shaking his head in wonder. "What were you thinking about? How did you do it?"

Images, uncomfortable images, of the drifter framed in the doorway, circle time, and the children singing songs flitted across the screen in Jennifer's mind. She shook her head, as if to shake loose the memories that were at once terrifying and incredible. Was it a bad dream? Had it really happened?

"To be honest," she said, pausing to take a sip of water, feeling more fatigued than she ever had in her entire life, "I don't think I was thinking at all. In fact, I know I wasn't. I was just on some sort of autopilot."

"Well, your autopilot," Mack began, "or whatever you want to call it, saved a lot of lives."

Jennifer shook her head again. "It was a starter's pistol," she said. "Or a cap gun."

Mack glanced at Greenfield's chief of police, who was leaning against Mack's desk, observing the conversation. He kept his head slightly ducked, as if to apologize for his broad shoulders and imposing frame.

When he spoke, his voice was quiet and gentle. "It was a loaded .45. That wasn't any starter pistol."

Jennifer's jaw dropped. She sank more deeply into the sofa. Unbidden, the magnitude of what had happened—and what she had somehow prevented—assailed her, and she started to cry. She felt like a sandbag was slowly sinking down on her shoulders. One of the paramedics handed her a box of tissues, which she gratefully accepted.

"A loaded .45 ?" she asked, between small sobs. "You've got to be kidding! I just thought it was some sort of cheesy, fake gun."

"There was nothing fake about it," Mack said. "You're a hero."

"I… I just want to go home," Jennifer said. And then she asked in a small voice, "Is that possible?"

Mack and the chief of police glanced at one another.

"Of course," Mack said gently. "As I said, I want you to take the rest of the week off."

"No, no. I couldn't do that. I will be in tomorrow, but I just need to go home right now," Jennifer responded.

"I don't expect you to come in, but if you feel more comfortable keeping your normal routine, that's fine. You can let me know later. The chief definitely wants to have a conversation with you, but it can wait, can't it, Chief?"

The chief gave a small nod.

"Are the kids okay?" Jennifer asked. "Maybe I should go back—"

"Your kids are fine," Mack said reassuringly. "Half of them didn't even understand they were in any kind of danger. And the other half—well, you know kids. They're a lot more resilient than we are. We've called their parents in, and we'll see if they need any special care or attention. And they'll get it if they do. But they're all just playing normally. They really thought he was some guy you brought in for show and tell."

Show and tell, Jennifer thought. They really thought he was in the room for a reason. How did I ever get them to believe that?

Jennifer sighed. "I'm still trying to figure out where my mind went during that whole thing," Jennifer confessed. "I've got absolutely no idea how I did… whatever I did. I don't remember what I did."

Mack chuckled. "I've got a feeling," he replied, "that we'd all be better off if we could come from wherever you were coming from when you handled that situation so beautifully. I've got a feeling the world would be a better place."

One of the paramedics spoke up. "We'd like to check her vitals before you send her home, Mr. Johnson," he said. "If everything's normal, Ms. Albright, you can go home. But otherwise, we'd like to take you to the hospital, just to be safe."

Mack looked at Jennifer, who nodded.

"Do what you have to do," Jennifer said.

A paramedic took her blood pressure, pulse, and temperature. He was young, hardly more than twenty, and he watched her face with wide, admiring eyes as she handed the thermometer back to him. All her vital signs were normal.

"You're one cool customer," the paramedic said, clearly impressed. Poise was the last thing he expected to encounter in his line of work.

Mack grinned. "That she is," he said. "Jennifer, what if one of these kind gentlemen gave you a ride home? We'll get your car home later."

Jennifer thought for a moment, composed herself, and nodded. "That would be great," she said. "I don't feel like I've got the energy to drive right now."

"It'll be my honor," said the chief of police. "I want to hear every detail." He grinned. "You can even work the siren."

Jennifer nodded. "I wouldn't want to scare the kids." She thought for a moment. "What are you going to tell the kids? I was there, and now I went home."

"I'll think of something," Mack said reassuringly. "Let the chief take you home. You've had a long day, and it isn't even nine-thirty yet."

Jennifer agreed. Slowly, she eased off the couch, not entirely trusting that she was well enough to stand unassisted. But she was.

"I'm okay," she told the concerned paramedics.

"You're a very brave young lady," the chief said. "It's time to take you home."

Chapter 3

By the time Jennifer awoke from a four-hour nap, she was famous. Internationally famous.

But by the time she realized how famous she was, she was furious.

Jennifer turned off her cell phone and her home phone as soon as the chief of police had dropped her at her door. She collapsed on her bed, still not believing that the experience she had gone through was real. After a long, deep, dreamless sleep, she arose, turned on her cell phone, and checked her messages.

Her message box was full.

Her message box was never full.

"What the…" she began, her voice trailing off.

In addition to the phone calls, it looked as though there were sixty or eighty texts. She had never seen so many texts on her phone in her life.

"Why are so many people…" she began. Then she went over to the home phone on her message machine. It, too, was full.

Tentatively, she hit the "messages" button on her home phone. The first message was from her mother. "Hi, darling," the reassuring voice began. "Your father and I saw you on the news and we wanted to make sure you were okay. Call me."

The news? Jennifer thought. How could they have seen me on the news?

She went to the kitchen to make herself a cup of coffee, wondering what she was doing on the news. As she was pouring a steaming cup—black, no cream or sugar—into her mug, it dawned on her that the situation in the classroom this morning was exactly the kind of thing the news media loved: a heartwarming story of children in danger, saved by the quick thinking— although it wasn't really thinking, she decided—of a schoolteacher.

Uh-oh, she thought.

Jennifer grabbed a pen and paper and played the rest of the messages on her home phone and her cell phone, and then she scanned the texts. About a third of the calls were from family members and friends who had seen the story on the news, read about it on the Internet, or otherwise had become aware of the standoff in her kindergarten classroom.

"This is nuts," she told herself.

The other two-thirds of the messages were from news organizations, magazines, and even TV shows and movie producers. Everybody wanted to interview her. Everybody wanted to make her even more famous than she already was.

"This is insane," Jennifer said. An intensely private person, Jennifer rarely socialized even with the other teachers in the school. She had a few friends in town, but her parents and the rest of her family were a thousand miles away, as was the college she had attended, as was her partner in the last serious relationship she had had, which had ended three years ago, on her twenty-sixth birthday. There were times when she felt lonely, but the last thing she wanted now was to be launched almost instantaneously into the public eye.

"This is absolutely crazy," she told herself. And suddenly she realized that in a media culture like ours, she was going to be famous, whether she liked it or not, whether she cooperated or not.

With a sinking heart, she went to her computer and logged onto the Internet. There she was, to her horror, on the front page of Yahoo—or at least her college graduation picture. Her gaze lingered on the image. She couldn't help but think that eight years had passed since then, and while she had achieved her career goal—teaching for the most acclaimed elementary school principal in the country—the rest of her life had not gone the way the expectant twenty-one-year-old in the graduation photo, now splayed across the Internet, had expected.

It's funny how just looking at a picture of oneself from eight years earlier could trigger all those thoughts. No real relationship, not a lot of money in the bank, not much more going on in her life than teaching, as much as she loved teaching, going to the gym every day for an hour, and renting movies on NetFlix. Not exactly what the twenty-one-year-old version of herself, now staring happily out at her from Yahoo's home page, had in mind.

She clicked on the story and read about how she had successfully calmed down a homeless man, mentally ill with a history of violence, according to the report, and ushered him from her classroom. She learned in the story that the little boy, Austin, who had put his hand up to go to the bathroom, casually mentioned to Mack Johnson that Ms. Albright had in the classroom a man with a gun for show and tell, which was "really cool," in Austin's words. Upon hearing this story from Austin, Mack peeked in the door of Jennifer's classroom, saw that there was indeed a stranger present, and immediately called the police and paramedics.

The story concluded with the fact that the President of the United States was so impressed with her actions that he was planning on inviting her to visit and accept a medal as a national hero.

"I have to be dreaming," Jennifer told herself. "The President?"

She opened Google News and discovered, to her intense dismay, that she was the lead story and that more than five thousand stories about her had already been posted online around the world. She clicked on the list and saw that wire service reports about her actions had been posted in newspapers in Australia, China, Japan, Great Britain, everywhere. She was still staring in disbelief at the screen when the phone rang.

She didn't pick it up, but let it go directly to voice-mail. "It's Jen. Leave a message," she heard herself say on her outgoing message.

"This is Fred Tedesco once again, calling from Oprah. She'd like to have you on the show tomorrow. 312-517-8930."

Jennifer massaged her temple. Oprah? The White House? Japan? China? Australia? All she did was talk to the guy. It's what anybody would have done, right?

The thought came to Jennifer that a jog might clear the cobwebs out of her brain. Also, she just wanted to get away from her phones and the Internet. She went back to her bedroom in her two-bedroom townhome, which she had purchased three years earlier with a little help on the down payment from her parents, changed into light blue running shorts and a loose t-shirt, and headed to the front door. She opened the front door and suddenly heard a voice she didn't recognize yelling, "There she is!"

To her horror, she found herself looking at an entire city of TV trucks encamped in front of her town-home and a crowd of more than a hundred reporters, people with boom mikes, and TV cameras that had mushroomed on her lawn. The moment she opened the door, they pressed forward towards her, their cameras flashing. A cluster of microphones was suddenly pushed towards her face like a Valentine's Day bouquet in some twisted alternate universe. Before she was even able to process the scene before her, the reporters started shouting out a barrage of questions.

"What were you thinking when you saw the home-less guy?"

"How does it feel to be a hero?"

"How soon are you going to the White House?"

"Did you know the gun was loaded?"

Terrified, unable to utter a syllable, Jennifer scanned the unwelcome crowd, her eyes wide and her mouth frozen in a tight line of surprise. She made no reply to the continued shouts of questions, and quickly stepped back inside and slammed the door. She leaned against the door, panting, stunned by the onslaught of media attention she was receiving.

The one thing the presence of all of these re-porters, cameras, and microphones meant to her was that the whole thing wasn't a dream. She really had saved the lives of who knows how many of her kindergarten students.

And perhaps her own as well.

But now she had an even bigger problem—she was a prisoner in her own home! She tiptoed through the townhome to the back door and peered out the window.

No one was there.

Maybe they didn't realize she had a back door.

She pulled her hair into a ponytail, put on a bulky sweatshirt that had belonged to her previous boyfriend, and grabbed a baseball cap and sunglasses. She headed out the back door, glanced furtively in both directions to make sure that she wasn't being observed, and then she made a dash for it. But as the door locked behind her, she suddenly realized she had no idea where to go. She had gone out without her keys, cell phone, or wallet.

She paused for an instant on the sidewalk that ran behind her townhome. But an instant was all the swarm of journalists needed. Suddenly a couple of photographers who had been smoking cigarettes in the alley alongside her home noticed her.

"There she is!" One of them yelled. They grabbed their cameras.

"Jennifer!" They shouted. "Over here! Look this way! Give us a smile, Jennifer! How does it feel to be a star?" They started shooting pictures of Jennifer, who couldn't figure out how they had recognized her, and then suddenly she got a grip on herself. Of course they know who I am, she told herself. They know exactly what they're looking for. Panicked, she started to run, but before she had gotten more than half a block away from her townhome, more and more reporters, photographers, and men with TV cameras had joined the hunt. Jennifer could feel her heart racing and her terror mounting. She felt her throat tighten like a vice was closing around her neck. Turning to look over her shoulder, she could see the entire pack of reporters in hot pursuit—dozens and dozens of reporters, photographers, and camera people—all shouting her name.

To Jennifer, this was an even bigger nightmare than the classroom. She didn't want the attention, she had no idea what she would say to them, and the idea of being engulfed by a sea of flashing lights and descending boom mics seemed to her to be a fate worse than drowning. Ahead of her was a busy intersection,

and the light had just changed so that a pack of ac-
celerating cars blocked her way. To her right was a gas
station where an enormous Suburban had just pulled
up to a pump and cut off her path. For a moment,
Jennifer stood looking to either side, caught in a rush
of frustration and fear, wrestling with her thoughts.

Then, suddenly, everything shifted. Jennifer found
herself going into that same mode of non-thinking
that had preserved her during the confrontation with
the gunman. The light in front of her changed again,
and she saw a man her age in a convertible pulling
up to the intersection. He looked okay. The moment
he stopped, she grabbed the passenger door without
thinking and pulled on it. The man looked at her in
surprise, but his expression softened almost immediately.

"It's locked," he said, not quite understanding why
a woman wearing an oversized sweatshirt, sunglasses,
and a baseball cap was trying to get into his car. Of
course, sweatshirt or not, he couldn't help thinking
that this would-be intruder was actually quite lovely—
in a tousled sort of way.

The light turned green. Jennifer considered her
options. Fueled by adrenaline, she hurled herself over

the locked passenger door and into the front seat. The man drove off, glancing sideways at her like she was some kind of alien creature that had just fallen from the sky.

"You'd better put a seat belt on," he said. "I don't want to get a ticket."

"That's the least of my worries," Jennifer said. "By the way, my name's Jennifer."

"I know," the man said. "I'm a TV writer. My name is David. Nice to meet you."

Jennifer blinked a few times, looking at him. He was wearing a crisp collared shirt and what looked like designer jeans, and his brown hair was closely cropped and styled neatly with gel.

"You're not here because of me, are you?" She asked him slowly, beginning to put two and two together.

"Heard your story and got on the first plane," David said.

Jennifer shook her head.

"I don't know who you are," she said wearily. "You just looked like a nice guy. All I ask is that you get me away from that pack of jackals behind me."

David smiled. Having run with that pack before, he was all too familiar with the accuracy of the description. "It might be better," David said, "if we put the top up." He pulled over and punched a button, and the top of the convertible rose up and clicked into place. "You're going to need all the privacy you can get."

Jennifer sighed. "You got that right," she said. "What did you say your name was again?"

David glanced down at Jennifer's running shoes as he started to drive on.

"Did you expect to outrun the media?" he asked wryly. "And it's David."

Jennifer made a face. "To be honest," she replied, "I was only hoping to go out for a jog. Clear my head. The last thing I expected was that I'd be all over the news, or that they'd be all over my front lawn."

"They're not gonna go away until you give them what they want," David said, eyes fixed on the road.

"What do they want?" Jennifer asked, confused. "They've got the whole story all over the news already."

"They've got the story of what happened," David corrected, "but they don't have your story."

Jennifer stared at him. "What do you mean?" she asked, alarmed. Her private nature was kicking in. "What do they want to know about me? And why?"

"It's kind of a competition," David said. He passed a hand over his hair and gave her an apologetic half-smile. "Who can put together the most comprehensive portrait of you. Who can talk to the most relatives, friends, coworkers, even your students. I'll bet Entertainment Tonight is sitting in the living room of the little boy who went to the bathroom, getting his story down."

Jennifer shuddered with revulsion. "They're even bothering the children?" she asked, outraged. "This is terrible! This is disgusting!"

"There's another name for it," David said calmly.

"What's that?" Jennifer asked.

"Reality," David said. "In case you haven't noticed, reality is what people like better than anything else. Reality TV, the reality of people's stories—stories like yours." He laughed. "Everybody likes other people's reality. It's kind of strange, but reality is the ultimate escapist genre today. And you're the new star."

Jennifer wanted to cry. She was just minding her own business, teaching her class, when this crazy situation arose, and now her own privacy was being sacrificed to satisfy—what? The hunger of people for a good story? That was one thing. But that they would bother the children in her class—that was just unacceptable.

She thought for a moment. "What do I have to do to make this whole thing go away?" she asked. Part of her felt a little jolt of surprise to hear her own voice come out high and plaintive. "I can't even go for a run. I'm locked out of my house. I've got no money on me, and I haven't even eaten anything since breakfast. I can't live like this."

Jennifer slumped ever so slightly in the front seat, but David caught it. He felt a sudden urge to protect her. "Let's get you something to eat," he said, studying the restaurant signs. "I think we could get a soup and a salad over there. How does that look?"

"It looks fine," Jennifer said. "I don't even know this part of town. I never come here."

"That's good," David said approvingly. "In that case, the media isn't likely to look for you here." He signaled and pulled into the parking lot of the restaurant.

Jennifer shook her head. "It's like this guy committed a crime by coming into my classroom," she reasoned, "but I'm the one they're chasing. But you didn't answer my other question. How do I get this whole media thing off my back, so that I can live my life?"

David pulled the car into a parking space. He thought for a moment how to answer her question.

"You can sell an exclusive on your story," he said finally. "Then the others will all back off. Rules of the game."

"This game has rules?" Jennifer asked, realizing that this situation was completely outside the bounds of anything she'd ever experienced before.

David grinned. "And some people even follow them," he said. "Let's get something to eat."

Suddenly Jennifer realized just how hungry she was.

"Best offer I've had all day," she said.

"I've got a feeling," David said, opening the door of his car and glancing back at Jennifer, "that the offers are about to get better and better."

Chapter 4

David and Jennifer found a table, ordered, and sipped the coffee the waitress brought them. The restaurant was nice enough—an Italian family place that was fairly quiet, since it was mid-afternoon. In fact, David and Jennifer were practically the only diners in the place. In a far corner, an older couple was passing the newspaper back and forth over their table. The waitress sat a few tables away, rolling silverware and glancing at Jennifer, who was a celebrity not just nationally but in her home town.

Jennifer could feel the quiet atmosphere and warm coffee slowly relaxing her. She rested her elbows on the tabletop and put her chin in her hands. "I could eat a horse," she admitted.

David grinned. "I hope that's not on the menu here!" he teased.

"Very funny," Jennifer said. "By the way, how do you know so much about the media works?"

"I've been part of it my whole professional career," David said. "I used to be a cameraman in hot spots. War zones, famines, some of the worst places on Earth. I guess I was looking to learn something about myself."

"And what was that?" Jennifer asked, interested.

"That I have absolutely no stomach for the sight of blood," David admitted ruefully. "I thought I was some kind of tough guy. I was wrong."

"So what did you do then?"

"Went to Hollywood," he said. "My news background helped me catch on as a third assistant director on a feature, and after a few years I gradually worked my way up the food chain until I was second assistant."

He grinned again. "That's when I knew that the production side wasn't where I wanted to be. That's when I got into writing."

"Writing what?" Jennifer asked, sipping her coffee

and grateful to be focused on something other than her own problems, like how she was going to get back into her home without any keys, and how she was going to run the gauntlet of media people encamped outside her home.

"Features," David said. "Action-adventure stuff. Except that didn't work, either. I wrote eleven scripts in two years, and sold none of them. Fortunately, I had a friend who worked in television production, and he brought a couple of my scripts into his producer, and that got me a gig writing feel-good TV movies for cable. You know, stuff with dogs and happy endings."

David raised one eyebrow ironically, as if to say, "Look what my great talent has been reduced to."

"Hey, I watch that stuff," Jennifer said.

"Fortunately, you're not alone," David replied. "I developed quite a niche for myself in that area, and I suddenly got hot. Now I write about ten movies-of-the-week a year, and none of them are on spec."

Jennifer cocked her head to the side, as if to ask what the term meant.

"Oh," David said, realizing that Jennifer didn't understand what he was saying. "On spec means you just write the script and hope that somebody buys it.

Once you get your foot in the door, you start getting assignments, where people are telling you, 'Here's the story to write, and by the way, here's a check.'"

Jennifer grinned. "That sounds pretty good."

"It is," David said. "It's allowed me to indulge myself in some of my favorite hobbies."

"Such as?"

"Eating," David said, chuckling. "And sleeping indoors. And paying the phone bill. Actually, it's a lot better than that. I've been very fortunate."

"Sounds that way," Jennifer said, just as the waitress was setting an enormous Caesar salad in front of her. Jennifer smiled up at her gratefully, then turned back to David. "So what brings you to Greenfield? I mean, this isn't exactly Hollywood."

Jennifer had barely gotten a fork into her salad when David candidly replied, "I told you already. You. You're what brought me here."

Jennifer's sinking feeling returned. She put her fork down. "Me?" she asked weakly.

"You," he said. "You're the ultimate feel-good story of the year. Of the decade. Maybe of the century. It's been a pretty slow century for feel-good stories."

"I am not a story," Jennifer said insistently. "I'm a kindergarten teacher, and there was a situation that somehow got handled. It's five minutes out of my life. It doesn't define me."

"It does to the media," David countered. "Five or ten minutes is all it takes to make—or break—a reputation. Actually, I think everything that you are was demonstrated in those five or ten crucial minutes. Your courage. Your desire to protect the children, which demonstrates your character. And above all, your ability to tap into some part of you that you might not even have ever known existed, someplace beyond thought, where you just almost instinctively do exactly what the situation commands."

Jennifer stared at him. "How do you know that much about what went on in the classroom this morning?" she asked. She realized her voice sounded harsher than she intended, but she was astonished to hear her experience so accurately described by someone she'd met hardly a half hour before. "Were you there?"

David shook his head and dipped his spoon into his soup. "The seventh grade English teacher—I think his name was Martland—sold his story to US Magazine for $250,000," he said. "He was just talking about

what you said when you were in the principal's office
when the whole thing was over."

Jennifer's blood boiled. "That's outrageous!" she
said. "How dare he!" She caught herself and sighed.
"What are you gonna do?" she added in a softer voice.
"I guess if you offer somebody that much money,
they're going to take it."

"Would you take it?" David asked, sounding as casual as he could. "Two hundred fifty thousand dollars
for your story?"

"No," Jennifer said dismissively. "There is no story.
I mean, it's over. And if the whole thing's already on
the media, and Mr. Martland has already sold his story,
then there's nothing left to tell."

"If there's nothing left to tell," David replied, taking another bite of his salad, "then why is every media
outlet in the world either already in Greenfield or on
its way here, ready to tell your story to a breathless
world?"

"The world ought to take a breath," Jennifer snapped.
"We're talking about the privacy of schoolchildren."

"We're talking about an astonishing act of brav-
ery," David said matter-of-factly. "An ordinary person
thrust into an extraordinary situation and relying on

her deepest self to save lives, including quite possibly her own." He paused, watching her. Jennifer was vaguely aware that she was scowling and drumming her fingertips nervously on the edge of the table. She didn't meet his eye. Instead, she stared across the restaurant at the older couple, who were chatting peacefully over their coffee mugs.

"You'd better eat something," David's gentle voice broke through her thoughts. "We could change the subject until you get some food into your system. I wouldn't want to be thinking about these things on an empty stomach."

Jennifer was about to tell him to mind his own business when she realized he was right. Her appetite had vanished as she contemplated the fact that she had become an object of scrutiny for the media and for the world, but she knew she had to eat something. She speared several leaves of lettuce, and with the first bite she realized just how hungry she was.

David said nothing, waiting for her to eat and get some of her strength back. He didn't want to push her for a story, but at the same time, he found her story to be remarkably inspiring. And she didn't seem to realize just how remarkable it was, which made it all the more remarkable. Plus, he had to admit…he was kind of enjoying her company, too.

"So that whole pack of jackals," Jennifer began, "will vanish if I sell my story as an exclusive to some-one?"

David gave an expansive shrug. "Pretty much," he said. "It may take a day or so for everybody else to back off, but they will."

"So who do I sell my story to?" Jennifer said. "What do I do, just go stand on the front lawn and sell my story to the highest bidder?"

David grinned again. "If you're going to do that," he said, "you'll want to sell the rights to that moment first, so nobody can put it on YouTube without your permission. That in and of itself would command a pretty penny."

"Seriously," Jennifer said. "I don't know anything about how any of this works. Who exactly am I sup-posed to sell my story to?"

"Me," David said, through a mouthful of Italian bread. Might as well go for it, he decided.

"You?" Jennifer repeated, surprised. "You're a TV writer—Oh. You're a TV writer."

"And I've got a cell phone, and I'm not afraid to

use it," David added, taking out his cell phone and putting it on the table next to his coffee cup.

"I really don't like it when people use cell phones in restaurants," Jennifer said.

"How does your boyfriend deal with that?" David asked, teasing her. "Sounds like there are a lot more rules where that came from."

"I don't have a boyfriend," Jennifer admitted.

"Just as well," David said. "He'd probably be negotiating to sell the rights to your story to cut a deal before you do."

"Probably," Jennifer said. "So what happens with this magical cell phone of yours?" she asked.

"I call my producer," David explained, "I tell him who I'm having lunch with, and he gives me the go-ahead to make you an offer for the exclusive rights to your story. It's pretty much that simple."

"And then everybody clears off my front lawn?" Jennifer asked, wanting to believe it.

"Pretty much," David said, buttering another piece of Italian bread. "Man, the bread is great here. Just like Musso and Frank's."

"How did I even end up in your car?" Jennifer asked. "That's kind of a blur to me, too."

"I was just driving along, minding my own business. When suddenly a beautiful woman in a jogging outfit hurtled the passenger side door. It was clearly meant to be."

Jennifer shot him a rueful look. "How do you know it was meant to be?" she asked.

"I don't," David admitted. "But where I come from, everybody's always saying things happen for a reason. Look, you've got to trust someone. It might as well be me."

Jennifer still couldn't figure it out. "You just happened to be driving through my town?"

David shook his head. "I didn't just happen to be driving through your town. I came here to look for you, so I could make you an offer on the exclusive rights to your story."

Jennifer shook her head. "That's quite a coincidence," she said. And then she thought back to how the morning had gone, when something other than her own will was dictating events. "Or maybe there are no coincidences."

"I can always drive you back home to the pack of jackals, as you so charitably put it," David replied.

Jennifer shuddered. As repellant as the idea of

seeing the crowd of reporters was to her, the complicating factor was that she still didn't have keys. She'd either have to get a locksmith to let her in while the crowd of photographers snapped pictures, or wait for a neighbor of hers who had a spare set of keys to her place.

Maybe things are happening for a reason, Jennifer told herself.

"How much are we talking about?" she asked, her tone slightly sarcastic. "After all, if Mr. Martland got 250K for his story, then surely mine would be worth…"

David cut her off. "A million dollars," he said calmly, popping a piece of buttered Italian bread into his mouth.

Jennifer laughed. "Don't play games," she said. "I'm really in no mood."

"I'm not playing a game," David said, through a mouthful of bread. "If I call my producer and tell him that I'm sitting with you—I mean, come on. I could call anyone in Hollywood and get you a million dollars for your story. Anyone."

"And that whole tribe of camera people will go away?"

"In a twinkling," David promised. "Okay, two twinklings. But yes, they'll go away."

"And you're not pulling my leg?" Jennifer asked, looking David straight in the eye. "You would really give me a million dollars for my story?"

"I wouldn't," David said, "but the producer I write for would. As would pretty much anyone in the entertainment industry. And then I would have the privilege of writing the TV movie."

Jennifer looked appraisingly at him. "What would that involve?" she asked.

David shrugged. "Hanging out in town for a few days, following you around to see what your life is like, maybe visit your school—when the kids aren't there. I think one stranger is enough for them for right now. But just get a feel for who you are, interview people who know what happened, that kind of thing. No big deal."

Jennifer paused, chewing her salad thoughtfully and weighing the potential intrusion of one person, admittedly a decent person for someone who claimed to work in Hollywood, for a few days, versus the media encampment that would follow her for who knows how long, until the story died down.

"Just three days?" she asked.

"And not a day longer," David promised. "At which point I would decamp for the glory that is Hollywood."

"Very funny," Jennifer said. And only then did she begin to ponder what the money would mean to her. At twenty-nine, by carefully putting aside 10 percent of her salary for the last six years, she had accumulated the magnificent sum of... $25,000 in her IRA. It might have been $25,000 more in savings than the average person, but if she ever wanted to move out of her townhome and buy a house, or retire one day, or do anything, whether she ever got married or not, a seemingly dubious proposition given her experiences with men up to this point, it was going to take a lot more than her tiny nest egg.

On the other hand, she felt as though she would be selling the children out by taking the money. It was their story as much as hers. They were the ones who were possibly traumatized by the ordeal they had undergone. Why should she get the money?

And then, on the other hand, to live with all those reporters and cameramen camped outside her home, following her to work, probably bothering her children and the neighbors and everyone else in her life…

"Two point one million," she countered. "I know there's probably some hefty tax and legal issues involved — which I'm sure your people will easily sort out. So, after tax and legal expenses, one hundred thousand to me and two million to be divided among the families of the children in my class, to be set aside for their college educations."

David studied her with a new expression on his face—respect. Not that he hadn't respected her all along, but he had never expected her to be such a shrewd negotiator. He couldn't help thinking to himself how Jennifer Albright was clearly full of surprises…and each of them more pleasant than the next.

"Let me make a phone call," he said, and then he added, in a teasing voice, "if you don't think it's too rude to make a phone call while I'm eating in a restaurant with you."

Jennifer made a face at him and gestured that he should go ahead and make the call.

David picked up his phone, punched in a number, and waited.

"Tom, it's me. You're not going to believe this. I'm sitting right here with Jennifer Albright, and she'll give us an exclusive on her story for a TV movie for two point one million dollars."

Jennifer waited expectantly, certain that the offer would be rejected and that this mysterious voice on the other end of the line would instruct David to counter for even less than Mr. Martland received.

"That's great," David said, grinning. He gave Jennifer a small nod, as if to say, "Done deal."

Jennifer's jaw dropped.

"Do me a favor," David was saying. "Have somebody go to my place and send me some clothes. I'll be here for a few days. You can fax me the agreement at my hotel, and I'll get a bank account number for a wire transfer. Oh. Two million is going into trust for the kids. So you'll want to get Legal on that, so they can figure out how to make out the check....I know. It is pretty cool. Call you later."

David disconnected and put his phone down.

"Congratulations," he said, extending a hand. "We have a deal."

Uneasily, Jennifer reached for his hand, which was surprisingly warm. She somehow expected a Hollywood TV writer to be a cold-blooded creature, like an eel or a viper or some other animal she taught her

children about in kindergarten. Instead, he had rescued her from a mob of hungry reporters and brought
her to this safe haven, complete with Caesar salads
and trust funds for her young students. She held his
hand for an extra-long moment, hoping that she had
made the right decision.

Chapter 5

As David drove her home, Jennifer felt her throat grow dry with dread and irritation. She still wasn't sure how she would get inside her locked door, even if she were able to push through the thick swarm of questions and flash bulbs that was guarding it.

But to Jennifer's intense surprise, when David turned onto her cul-de-sac, the street looked eerily normal. The overwhelming majority of the reporters, TV cameras, and men carrying boom microphones had melted away, like snow in August. Where had they gone? How did they know that their services were no longer required? She hadn't seen David make any more telephone calls than the initial one that had confirmed her deal.

There was obviously a lot about this world she didn't know.

And didn't need to know, she told herself. Three days with this man, giving him access to her life, whatever that meant, and telling her story, and the whole thing would be over. And then, if she was lucky, she wouldn't have any more contact with Hollywood for the rest of her life, aside from going to see a movie—a movie not about her—at the local multiplex.

"You've been very kind," Jennifer said sincerely. "I really don't know how you got all these people to go away."

"Word travels fast," David explained, cutting the motor on his car. "Once people heard you had signed an exclusive, they knew there was nothing to talk about. Those are kind of the rules of the game."

Jennifer thought for a moment, studying the mess the media had made on her lawn—fast food wrappers, cigarette butts, cups left behind, the detritus of a small but not insignificant army.

"It's hard to believe there are any rules," she mused.

And then she thought of something. "I haven't signed anything yet."

David glanced at her, admiring her ability to play hardball. "We have an agreement," he said. "In Hollywood, verbal agreements aren't worth the paper they're not printed on, but I have a feeling you'll be true to your word."

Jennifer nodded. "So what's the plan?"

"You get some sleep," David said softly, not without some compassion for the ordeal she had gone through. "Then, in the morning, you and I get started."

Jennifer put up her hands. "In the morning," she interrupted, "I go to work. I have a job. Remember?"

David thought for a moment.

"All right, when you get home from work. At that point, I'll have a contract for you to sign, and the check. And then we start rolling."

"A check?" Jennifer asked, surprised. "It happens that fast?"

"It happens that fast," David said. "I'm honestly grateful to have the opportunity to tell your story. I think we're going to inspire a lot of people."

Jennifer shrugged. "It's hard to believe that a TV movie could inspire anything," she said, her tone sarcastic. She watched as the wind blew an empty cigarette package left by the reporters lazily across the driveway. "To be honest, I'm just doing it for the money for the kids. They ought to get something for what they went through. I mean, if Mr. Martland is making money on this thing, why shouldn't they?"

David grinned. He'd only known Jennifer for an hour, but he liked her style more and more.

"Thanks to your excellent negotiating skills," he said, "I think the kids have done just fine in the deal. Don't you?"

Jennifer smiled back. "I think so," she said. And then she turned serious. "I haven't even thought of them all day. I've just been so consumed with what happened to me, with all this media insanity. I hope they're okay."

David gave her a reassuring smile. "I'm sure they'll be fine. Have a good night."

Jennifer nodded at him, opened the car door, and said, "I guess we can meet back here around four. Is that okay?"

David nodded. "Perfect," he said.

He waved as she stepped out of the car. As she shut the door behind her, she looked over her shoulder and caught his eye one last time. They smiled at one another. As David shifted out of neutral, he found himself surprised—and a little delighted—by how much he was looking forward to the next day. He hadn't felt that way about a job in a long time...if ever.

Jennifer headed across the lawn to her neighbor's house to pick up her spare key. She heard David's convertible driving off just as two photographers, who must not have gotten the memo that she had signed (or was about to sign) an exclusive deal for the rights to her story, ran up. They took a few pictures, but Jennifer barely paid any attention to them. She was too tired to care.

Thankfully, her neighbor answered the door almost immediately after Jennifer rang the bell. He was a stout, middle aged man who had never married. Though he was fairly reserved, he had always been friendly to Jennifer and always picked up her mail when she went home to visit her parents. He smiled at her without a trace of curiosity in his eyes when he handed her the keys, saying simply, "I can only imagine the day you've had."

Jennifer laughed. "Like you wouldn't believe," she agreed.

She let herself into her place, and without even undressing or brushing her teeth, she fell onto her bed into a deep and dreamless sleep.

Chapter 6

The next morning, Jennifer awoke without an alarm. A band of sunlight was peeking in through the curtains on the window above her bed, and it fell across her stomach in a sharp line. Jennifer looked down at it and was for a moment baffled to find that she was still in running clothes. Then the totality of the events of the day before sprang into her mind, and her first thought was panic. She sat bolt upright in bed and said out loud, "The kids! I hope they're okay!"

Jennifer hurried through her morning routine, showering, and dressing simply in brown slacks and a soft, violet sweater. She downed a piece of wheat toast with almond butter and half a cup of black coffee before she scooted out the door and drove, a little too quickly, to school.

To her immense relief, if there had been media at the school, they, like their brethren at her home, had moved on, too. It pretty much looked like a day just like any other. The parking lot was slowly filling as teachers parked their cars and grabbed shoulder bags full of books and lesson plans. Many of them waved at her or smiled reassuringly, but no one approached her. Jennifer was grateful. Maybe Mack asked them to give me some space for awhile, she thought.

And just as she thought of him, the principal ambled into view.

He looked solicitously at Jennifer. "I wasn't sure if you'd be coming in today," he said. "I actually lined up a sub."

Jennifer looked at him as if he were crazy.

"I'm fine," she insisted. "What happened yesterday is over. At least for me." But she couldn't help wondering if she were somewhat in denial about how powerful the events of the day before had been.

"Well, I'm okay enough to teach," she added.

Mack studied her. "You sure?"

"I'm sure," she said. "Have you sold your version of the story anywhere?"

Mack gave her a rueful look.

"Not even tempted to," he said flatly. "And I've turned down some big money. Believe you me." Then his expression changed, and he gave her a solemn smile. "Hey, I heard about what you did for the kids. That's beautiful."

"How did you hear about it?" Jennifer asked, surprised.

"A two million dollar trust fund for the college education of your students? That was quick thinking, young lady. We were all mightily impressed." And then he shook his head. "Unlike our fabled English teacher, Mr. Martland," he said. "Selling a story for a quarter-million dollars. It's no secret that teachers are underpaid – the temptation was clearly too great for him to resist."

The two of them exchanged a smile and Jennifer headed to the classroom. Seeing Mack gave her just the touch of normalcy she needed to get her day started the right way.

When she entered her classroom, a few of the children were already present, supervised by one of the class moms, who had wanted to make sure that everything would be okay the next day. Several of the children jumped up and crowded around Jennifer, and one of the little girls waved a drawing of a cat she had made. Jennifer laughed and put her hand on the little girl's red curls. "Beautiful, Tiffany!" She exclaimed. "Now everyone take your seats, please. It's not quite time to begin—let's wait for the rest of the class."

The class mom, who happened to be the mother of Austin, the boy who had gone to the bathroom, smiled and nodded at Jennifer. "Good morning," Jennifer said, smiling back and beginning to put her things down on her desk.

"Here's the hero of the day," the mother said to the children, grinning widely. Then she walked over to Jennifer's desk and continued quietly, "Thank you for what you did yesterday. In the classroom, and then with the money. It's all so hard to believe."

Jennifer shrugged and ducked her head. "I'd like to take credit," she said, "but it just seemed like something took over in me. Anyway, it's a new day. How are the kids?"

A few more kindergartners arrived at the door, pulling their backpacks behind them, giggling amongst themselves. They crowded around their cubbies and began hanging their sweaters up, as Jennifer had taught them. They looked pretty unscathed, to Jennifer's eye.

"I think the kids are okay," the mom said. "They probably got more bothered by the media attention than by the gunman. I don't know if you know this, but there were reporters at every child's house when we got home from school. Reporters and cameramen. It was like a mini-circus at every house of every family in the class."

Jennifer shook her head. The media. "I had no idea," she said, disgusted.

The woman nodded ruefully. With one hand, she swept her hair, fine and blonde like Austin's, away from her face. Jennifer noticed that her expression was clear, her eyes unclouded. For a moment, she felt almost overwhelmed to see how happy the woman looked. They could both so easily have awoken to a very different reality that morning.

"We won't ever be able to thank you enough," the woman said, interrupting Jennifer's reverie. She shook Jennifer's hand warmly, waved at Austin, and slipped out the door.

She glanced at the round, sweep-second clock on the wall.

"Okay, class," she said, in her most reassuring tones. "Circle time. Does anybody want to talk about what happened yesterday?"

"Is our new friend coming back?" one of the children asked as they gathered in a semicircle on the story carpet around Jennifer.

Jennifer shuddered. "I hope not," she said. "Actually, I don't think so. I don't think we're ever going to see him again."

The day proceeded smoothly. In circle time, Jennifer gently drew the children into a short conversation about the previous day's events. A couple of them shyly told her that they had been frightened, but when she asked them to talk more about it, they seemed less affected by the gunman than by the thrill of seeing their school on TV while their parents watched the news during dinner. Other than that, the resiliency of children to absorb an unusual situation and keep on going demonstrated itself. Before long, the children were sitting at their seats, absorbed in the day's lesson—rainforests. As Jennifer handed out papers and crayons for them to draw pictures of monkeys and toucans, she felt confident that they had put all, or at least most, thoughts of the gunman out of their minds.

Not so for Jennifer, who remembered as the day came to a close that she would have to meet David and talk about the whole thing. For a brief moment, she was tempted to call him and say bluntly that she had changed her mind, but she had given her word, and on top of that, there was the rich financial bonanza for the kids. It seemed that they and their parents had begun to get wind of the news, and all she had to do to make good on it was show up and talk. Beyond that, Jennifer was beginning to feel convinced that David wasn't such a bad guy, even though he was part of the media, whom by now she considered to be the enemy for its ruthlessly intrusive and obtrusive nature.

As she made her way across the teachers' parking lot at the end of the day, she began to feel truly anxious. What would she say during her meeting with David? What kind of questions was he going to ask? Would her life seem boring and unimportant? A million different fears and worries gnawed away at her as she began the drive home, both hands tightly gripping the steering wheel.

But after a few minutes, something strange happened. As her car glided smoothly down the road, Jennifer felt a sense of calm that felt foreign yet familiar. The streets were pleasantly traffic-free, and for the first time that spring, she noticed that the trees on either side of the road were in full bloom, dotted with fresh pink and ivory blossoms. Without effort, Jennifer found herself for a few moments allowing everything to be exactly as it was. As she allowed it, all the tightness in her muscles began to dissolve, and she looked down at her hands on the steering wheel to see that the color had returned to her knuckles. It was as if her whole body had loosened its hold.

Then, urged by some unknown force from within herself, she took a deep breath. The air filled her lungs and gave her the sensation of weightlessness. She took another breath and exhaled, and then another. A sense of calm permeated her being each time her chest expanded and contracted with a breath. Jennifer, who was always thinking and over-thinking, was surprised to find her mind completely devoid of thought. Even the world speeding by outside her car was unusually silent, instead of bombarding her with distractions like it usually did. She felt almost like liquid, as if she had tapped into a universal flow of peace and well-being. For a moment, time seemed to suspend in mid-air while she coursed along an inexplicable current of simply being.

This is exactly what it felt like in the classroom yesterday, she realized. This is how I felt when I saw the gun.

With a strange sense of wonder, she rode the flow all the way home.

Before she knew it, she was turning into her driveway. And there was David, waiting in front of her townhome at four o'clock, just as he'd promised. He was leaning on the side of his red convertible, flipping through the pages of a small notepad.

In a flash, her feeling of inner peace evaporated and all of the same worries and fears flooded back into her consciousness. Her whole life had changed when that man came into her classroom, and she'd never asked for it to. Why couldn't things go back to normal? She looked at David, who looked rather handsome standing beside his shiny car, and felt a surge of inadequacy. What if he decided the story wasn't good enough for a TV movie after all?

Suddenly, Jennifer longed for the feeling of contentment she had just experienced with every ounce of her being. It had been so wonderfully freeing not to think, and she couldn't help but notice how effortlessly she'd allowed external circumstances to suck her back into fretting and over-analyzing. Maybe there's a way to sustain that feeling, she thought as she turned off her car engine. Maybe there's some way to allow things to be just as they are, no matter what. But the question is: how?

She shook her head and sighed. I'll think about it later, she decided, as she took a deep breath and strode out of her car.

"Where's your television crew?" she asked David by way of greeting.

David shook his head. "And hello to you, too," he said, teasing her.

"Sorry, forgot my manners," Jennifer admitted. "I guess I'm a little nervous. I've never done anything like this before."

"I'll be gentle," David said, giving her a warm smile. "And right now, we're just doing background interviews. That's what we'll do over the next couple of days, and then maybe another time we'll go around a little bit with a film crew. If that's really necessary. But you've got to remember I'm writing a story about you that's going to be a TV movie. It's not a documentary. Somebody's going to play you in the movie."

Jennifer shook her head, trying to wrap her mind around that idea. "That sounds so bizarre," she murmured.

"You'll get used to it," he said. "I've got a feeling a lot of top actresses will be competing for the part. Anyway, is there someplace we can go talk?"

"There's a coffee shop a couple of blocks from here," Jennifer suggested.

"Sounds good to me," David said. "Let's go."

He opened the door of his convertible for her, then walked around to the driver's side. As he started the engine, he glanced at her and asked solicitously, "Strictly off the record—how are you doing?"

Jennifer couldn't help but smile. "Not bad. It was good to be back at school."

When they arrived at the coffee shop, Jennifer was pleased to see that it was just busy enough that they could blend in. It was a small, family-owned place, with five or six tables and a glass case filled with danishes and cupcakes. At Jennifer's suggestion, David got them both cups of chai—the house specialty. They carried their generously-sized mugs to a table in the corner and sat down.

"Aren't you going to tape-record me?" Jennifer asked, surprised to see that David was just taking out his pad and a pen.

"That's not how I work," he admitted. "No TV cameras, no digital recorder. I just like to sit and talk. Get to know somebody. Is that okay?"

And before Jennifer could answer, he touched his forehead, as if he had forgotten something.

"Oh, before I forget," he said. "Business before pleasure."

He reached into a jacket pocket and pulled out some legal documents. He put them on the table before Jennifer.

"What's this?" Jennifer murmured, but she knew what she was looking at. It was the agreement for the rights to her story. She skipped through a few pages of legalese, which neither interested nor troubled her, and skimmed until she found the part about the money. She read, "Two million dollar trust fund to be established in her name, for the benefit of the students who were in her classroom the morning of the situation in question."

While she had been reading, David had quietly taken out a cashier's check for $2 million, made out to a trust fund that had been created for the children's education.

Jennifer, like most people, had never seen a check for $2 million before in her life. She stared at the long line of zeroes. There were so many of them that they seemed to blend together and swim in her vision.

"Holy cow," she said.

"Yeah," David said. "It's a lot."

"A whole lot." Jennifer shook her head, as if she were trying to wake up from a dream she couldn't believe was real. It was no dream. It was a real check, and a real contract from a real studio. And then David took out a second check, in the amount of $100,000, payable to her; the taxes having already been covered.

"Where do I sign?" she murmured, amazed.

David indicated the signature line on the contract. Jennifer took a deep breath and signed her name.

She pointed to the checks. "May I take them?" she asked.

"You've earned them," David said, grinning. "Actually, you'll really earn over the next few days. But yes, you can."

Jennifer took two checks, studied them for a little while longer, unable to believe that they were real, shrugged, and put them in her purse.

She'd have to talk to somebody, maybe Mack Johnson, about finding a lawyer who could draw up the trust documents. She made a mental note to do that the next day. The idea of walking around with checks that big in her purse was a little more than she could absorb.

"Where do we begin?" she asked.

"Tell me about yourself," David said, and suddenly Jennifer laughed.

"I feel like we're on some sort of computer date," she blurted out.

David studied her. "What do you mean?" he asked. And then he got it.

"Oh. Here we are. Two strangers sitting in a coffee shop, and me saying, 'Tell me about yourself,' as if I were some sort of lame guy on a first date with you."

"Kind of," Jennifer said. "Is this how people go on dates in Hollywood?"

David gave a brief sigh. "I wouldn't exactly say that people in Hollywood go on dates," he said. "It's more like they get married and then they find out if they're compatible, and then they find they aren't, so they get divorced. But by then, they've either adopted sixteen kids or bought fourteen houses, or ended global warming, or all three, so it's a little more complicated than in the real world."

"I think I'll stick to my own life," Jennifer said.

"I'd like to hear about that life," David said warmly. And as he said it, he realized that he actually did want to hear about her life—and not just for the sake of making the movie, either.

Jennifer blushed. "This is a little embarrassing," she said, taking a sip of her chai. "I mean, I'm a kindergarten teacher. It's not like I'm some sort of exciting person. It's not like I write, I don't know, movies for TV."

David laughed. "In Hollywood," he explained, "there's nobody lower than the writers. Even the guards stationed in front of studios know they'll have a job tomorrow. Writers don't. We're the bottom of the barrel."

"Well," Jennifer said, "you seem to be the top of the bottom." And then she frowned. "That didn't come out the way I meant it to. No offense."

"No offense taken," David said. "So, have you always been a kindergarten teacher?"

"Not when I was seven years old," Jennifer countered. "I used to be a kid."

"Point taken," David said. "By the way, this isn't 60 Minutes. I'm just trying to get to know you."

"Well, this is me," Jennifer replied. "I'm just... it's just a little awkward for me to be talking about myself."

"Tell me about why you love kids so much," David said, taking a different tack. "You've got to love kids to take a job like yours."

Jennifer brightened. It was a lot easier for her to talk about her love of kids than about herself.

"My kids are amazing," she said. "I guess I've always loved kids, and I had great teachers when I was in school. I just always knew that I wanted to go into teaching, and especially working with small children."

"How come?" David asked, prodding her gently, although it took very little to get Jennifer to open up about her love for children.

"They're so cute," she said. "They're these little people—I mean, their bodies are small, but their spirits and their personalities are full-sized. Outsized, sometimes. And they've got this challenge of trying to figure out how to navigate the world, trying to figure out who they are, what it means to be a son or a daughter, a friend, a student in a classroom. I get to tell them about rainforests and ducks and how trees grow and where snow comes from. How to count. How to read. How to get along with others. It's the sweetest thing in the world."

David looked thoughtful as he pondered Jennifer's response. "I don't think I've ever heard anybody make a better case for teaching children," he said. "Usually, when you think about kindergarten, you just think about kids fighting, runny noses, maybe even some diapers that have to be changed."

Jennifer grinned. "Our kids are pretty much out of diapers," she said. "Not always, but that's not really a big deal."

"Maybe for you," David said. "I don't really see myself as a diaper-changing guy."

Jennifer grinned. "Men never do," she said. "But somehow they get the hang of it." And then she grew more serious.

"But that's not really what it's about. You don't even notice that stuff. It's about watching them grow. Not just physically, although that's amazing enough. They come in and their legs are short and by the end of the school year, they've gotten taller and more confident physically. That's sweet enough.

"But I mean watching their minds grow. Watching them change. Helping to facilitate that change. That's what I love about what I do. The hardest day of the year for me is the last day of school, because I love them so much and now they aren't mine anymore. I mean, I'll see them in school over the next few years, because we're K through six here, but it's not the same thing. The only good news is that I get a new group to be with, to love, really, the following September. I just have to hang in through the summer until they get there."

"It almost makes me want to quit what I do and teach kindergarten," David said, with evident sincerity. "Okay, emphasis on the word almost. But go on."

"That's really about it," Jennifer said. "I just love being with them. I love hearing what they have to say about the world, about each other, and even what they say about me. It's fun."

"What do they say about you?" David asked.

Jennifer grinned, and looked off in the distance, as if she weren't sure that she wanted to betray a secret.

"Sometimes they tell me they love me," Jennifer said. "Sometimes they tell me they want to marry me.

Sometimes they tell me they wish I could be their mommy. That's when I know something not so great is going on at home, and those are the moments that break my heart. That kind of thing."

She looked awkwardly at the floor, uncomfortable about sharing that level of intimacy with a near stranger. The bond she shared with her students was so strong that she had never really discussed any of this with anyone, even with Mack Johnson, who, she was certain, felt the same way.

"It's beautiful," David said, leaning slightly forward in his chair. "And it's perfect. You're really helping me understand the makeup of a really wonderful, dedicated kindergarten teacher, which is what you are."

"Thank you," Jennifer said in a small voice. "I'm just not used to talking about this kind of thing."

"Well, from my perspective, you're doing great," David said encouragingly.

"This isn't boring?" Jennifer asked, sounding doubtful. "Why a girl loves to teach kindergarten? I mean, I don't think you can get any more boring than that."

"That's not how it is for me," David said. "I think it's fantastic."

"Fantastic in a Hollywood, let's do lunch kind of way?" Jennifer asked, her eyes boring into him.

"No," David said putting up his hands in mock surrender. "We're not in Hollywood. We're here. In Greenfield. I can tell the truth."

"So that's the truth," Jennifer said. "What else?"

"What about you?" David asked. "I don't get the feeling you're married. Are you seeing anyone?"

"Do we really have to go there?" Jennifer said, somewhat defensively.

"I could say we have two million reasons to go there," David said, teasing her, "but the thing is that I'm trying to get a sense of what your life is like. I've got to create a role based on you for the TV movie. It doesn't have to be exactly your story, but I at least have to know what your story is. And I promise I won't ask anything that you consider too intrusive. If I do, I'll just back off."

"I'd be grateful for that," Jennifer said quietly. "I'm really a very private person, and talking about myself isn't exactly something that comes easily for me."

"There aren't too many like you in Hollywood," David said. "You can take my word for that. So. Are you married?"

Jennifer shook her head. David could sense that this was a sore point for her. He waited.

"I've come close a couple of times," Jennifer said, taking another sip from her mug. By now David had realized that she took a sip whenever she was feeling vulnerable or exposed.

"But nothing really worked out," she continued. "This is a great town to live in, but it's not exactly a mecca for single guys. It's actually kind of hard to meet people here."

"It's hard to meet people anywhere," David said. "I mean, people you could be serious about."

Jennifer gave a small shrug. "I can't speak for other places," she said. "But it seems like the way life is today, you go to work, maybe you go to the gym, you go to the supermarket, and you come home. There really aren't a lot of places to meet guys. To meet people."

"Sounds like you need to get out a little more," David said playfully.

Jennifer rolled her eyes. "I know," she said. "All my girlfriends tell me the same thing. But you're tired after the end of a day—I know people don't think it's true, but teaching kindergarten's hard work. If you're going to do it the right way, anyway, and pretty much everyone I know who does this, does it the right way. But then you come home and you're pretty wiped out, and you've got to create a lesson plan for the next day, and maybe there are some meetings after school, or a parent wants to talk to you. Parents are e-mailing all the time now. They've all got something to say about what's going on in the classroom. Which is good, I guess, but it definitely cuts into my own personal time, because you don't get to check your e-mail at school. Or at least not very often.

"So you come home, and I do try to get to the gym pretty much every day. But even at the gym, you see the same people, and it's not exactly a place where I feel comfortable talking to guys. Or maybe they don't feel comfortable talking to me."

"I know what you mean," David said.

Jennifer studied him, to determine if he was being empathetic or patronizing her. She decided he was serious, because he had already demonstrated his willingness to tease her, and he didn't appear to be teasing her now.

"So it's kind of a challenge," she concluded, "to meet guys. I just turned twenty-nine." She paused for a moment. "I never thought I'd be this old and not be married," she said. "What do you think about that? There's breaking news. 'Kindergarten Teacher Surprised To Be Single. Film at 11.'"

"We'll get that right into the headlines," David said, grinning. "I'm thirty-two. I could say the same thing about myself."

"Really?" Jennifer asked. "Since you're from Hollywood, I thought you'd have adopted 16 children by now and restored the ozone layer."

"Ha!" David chuckled, appreciating the truth behind her joke. She did have a point. "Well for now, let's just stick to you," he said, gently steering the conversation back in her direction. "So you thought you'd be married by now."

"I guess so," Jennifer said, "although I don't exactly see what this has to do with the story about the kids."

"It's a story about you," David politely reminded her. "We'll get to the kids. I promise. I just want to hear about you. I've got to—"

"Draw up a character based on me," Jennifer said, finishing his sentence before him. "I remember. So what more do you want to know?"

"So what do you do at night?" David asked. "It can't all just be the gym and drawing up lesson plans, and e-mailing parents over who spilled the finger paints onto what other kid's sweater."

"Well," Jennifer said, giving a rueful grin, "I guess there isn't all that much to my life. I guess you must be a little disappointed."

"I'm never disappointed by normal," David said. "Not after all the insanity I go through in my particular industry."

"Then why do you stay?" Jennifer asked him.

"I really haven't figured that one out," David admitted, marveling at how Jennifer had a knack for getting him to reveal more about himself with her than he did with anyone else. "But we were talking about you. Do you ever do online dating?"

Jennifer blushed deeply. "I do online lurking," she admitted. "I just, um… I just look at a lot of profiles, but I've never actually made contact with anybody."

David studied her. "Why not?" he asked. "What's the worst that could happen?"

Jennifer took another quick sip of tea. "You'd actually have to talk to them," she said. "You'd have to open up to a total stranger."

"Like you're doing right now," he said. "Although,

of course, they aren't paying two million for the right to have chai tea with you."

Jennifer rolled her eyes again.

"Maybe they should have to," David said, teasing her again. "You can put that in your profile. 'If you'd like to have tea, it'll cost you two million dollars. And even then, I'll only tell you what I feel like telling you.'"

"Very funny," Jennifer said, pretending to be annoyed. "I guess I'm just a little shy. Is that such a problem?"

"Only if you're twenty-nine and you want to be married," David said, and Jennifer glanced quickly at him to see if he was making fun of her.

He wasn't.

"I guess you're right," she said. "How are we doing so far?" she asked doubtfully. "Are you getting what you need?"

"More than I expected," David said. "I'm getting hungry. What about you? Or if chai tea is two million with you, is dinner four million?"

Jennifer gave him a grin. "You'll have to talk to my agent about that," she said. "But dinner sounds great. A working dinner, though. This isn't a date."

David put up his hands in mock surrender again. "Just doing my job," he said merrily. "Just doing my job. Actually, I already bought some dinner for us."

"You did?" Jennifer asked, startled. She looked around where David was sitting. "Where is it? What is it?"

David stood up and gave her a mysterious smile. "Follow me!" he exclaimed, and he escorted her out of the coffee shop and back to his car.

Chapter 7

It was a beautiful spring day, and David thought it would be a good idea to take advantage of the warm weather. He put the top down on his convertible and drove toward one of Greenfield's largest parks.

"Where are we going?" Jennifer asked, studying David, who drove and offered no clues.

"You'll see soon enough," he said. "Am I turning into a man of mystery for you?"

"You're a mystery, all right," Jennifer replied. "I hope I can trust you."

"Two million reasons to trust me," David cracked.

"Fair enough," Jennifer said, tossing her hair and making the decision to follow his lead and just go along with his plan. Unless it was too crazy, of course. Her mind drifted back to her classroom.

"I just can't get over how quickly kids get beyond stuff," she said. "What happens to us as we get older? We lose that ability to bounce back."

"That's a great point," David said. "I never thought about it, but it's true."

"I know it sounds like a cliché, but there's a lot you can learn from kids," Jennifer said.

"They surprise you, I'll bet."

"Yeah, they do," Jennifer said. "You know the little boy in my class who had to go to the bathroom?"

David nodded.

"This morning, he said the most amazing thing," Jennifer continued. "It really blew me away. He asked me if I had ever noticed that when you breathe, the air is cooler when it goes into your nose when you inhale than it is when you exhale."

David thought for a moment as he turned into the park. They were on a broad lane, bordered on both sides by enormous old trees that created a canopy of leaves above them.

"I never thought of that," he said, "but it makes sense. Unless you're in the tropics, or on a really sweltering day, your body temperature is going to be higher than the, what's it called, the ambient temperature. Is that the right word? I just mean the temperature of the air when you're walking around. So if you breathe in, you're taking in cooler air, and since it goes into your lungs and your whole system, it gets warmer—that's pretty amazing—I never thought of that."

"Me, neither," Jennifer said. "That's part of the reward of teaching little kids. You just never know what they're going to come up with. We had done a whole thing on the human body, about breathing, a couple of months ago. That's the other funny thing—when you teach kids something, you never know what sticks. You never know what stays in their minds or what they just kind of, I don't know, flush. But obviously I made a point with Austin."

David parked his car in a small lot tucked between the trees. They got out, and he popped open the trunk.

"I took the liberty," he said.

Inside the trunk was a picnic hamper.

"If we were doing this in Hollywood," he explained, as Jennifer looked on in surprise, "we'd be eating at some big fancy restaurant every day we were working.

Things are a little more low key here in Greenfield, but I figured it wouldn't hurt to have a nice meal."

Jennifer saw that David had brought a blanket and a complete dinner from the Italian restaurant where they had eaten the night before. They strolled for a few minutes down a path covered in soft pine needles until they came to an open, grassy area in the park. There was a large pond in the center of the clearing, and a gentle breeze blew ripples along the water. A father was sitting at the edge of water with his two small children, whom he was teaching to skip stones across the pond's surface. There were a few picnic tables scattered throughout the area, but David spread out the blanket on the ground under an enormous oak tree.

As they sat down, Jennifer wasn't sure what to say. She was touched by David's thoughtfulness.

"I hope you like lasagna," he said.

"This was really thoughtful of you," Jennifer said. "You really didn't have to do anything like this."

"I just thought it would make it feel less like work and more like, I don't know, just having a conversation."

David unwrapped the various dishes, handed Jennifer some silverware and a napkin, and uncorked a bottle of wine.

"The studio is paying," David said. "I thought we could live it up a little."

"Sounds good to me," Jennifer said. "By the way, the parents have been calling and e-mailing. They're really grateful to you for the trust fund for their kids' education. You solved a lot of problems with that one."

David shrugged, pouring the wine. "It's really you who did it," he said. "That trust fund idea was all yours. Just about anybody in your position would have taken the money and run."

Jennifer didn't respond. It would never have occurred to her to do it any other way. She accepted the glass of wine from David.

She thought for a moment.

"To the children," she said, raising her glass. "I guess that's why we're here."

"I'll drink to that," David said, and they clinked glasses and took a sip of the wine. It was surprisingly good, given the fact that the bottle cost $8.99 and was the most expensive bottle for sale at the restaurant. I guess I'm not in Hollywood anymore, David thought.

"I asked Austin what gave him that idea about the breathing," Jennifer said, as she took a bite of her lasagna. "His answer really surprised me."

David, busy with his lasagna, waited for more.

"He says he noticed when he saw the homeless guy in our classroom," Jennifer explained, a measure of awe in her voice. "It's really wild. He said that when he saw the gun, he was scared, and he realized that he stopped breathing for a moment. I mean, that's a pretty sophisticated thought for a five-and-a-half-year-old. But these kids can really surprise you sometimes with how, you know, wise beyond their years they can be.

"Anyway," Jennifer continued, "he said that all of a sudden he remembered our class about inhaling and exhaling, and as he inhaled, he noticed the difference. Can you imagine that?"

David said nothing. He put his fork down, and listened intently to Jennifer's story.

"He said that if he looked at the gun it would be too scary," Jennifer continued, "so instead, he just closed his eyes, and inhaled. And then when he exhaled, he noticed that the air going out of his nose was warmer than the air that had come in.

"So he did it again. He breathed in, and noticed that the air was cool, and then he breathed out, and he noticed that the air was warmer. He did that a bunch of times."

"And then what happened?" David asked, leaning forward.

"He said all of a sudden he realized he needed to go to the bathroom," Jennifer said, and they both laughed.

"That's when he put up his hand and told me he had to go, and I asked the homeless guy if it would be okay, and he said yes. I figured I might as well just check in with him because he probably didn't want any surprises. So he went to the bathroom, and obviously he must have told somebody, because the next thing you knew, the police were there."

Jennifer took another sip of wine. David waited.

"It's really amazing," she said. "I wonder if he would have noticed that he needed to go to the bathroom if he hadn't done that kind of breathing exercise. And then what would have happened? I mean, the police would never have known to come— it could have been much worse. It could have been really bad."

David took a sip of wine and shifted in his position on the picnic blanket.

"Are you saying that the little boy got...I don't know what you'd call it. In touch with himself? Is that what they call it? I really don't know much about that whole thing. I have friends who meditate, and do yoga, and stuff, but I never really got into it myself."

Jennifer reflected.

"It's really hard to say. You look back and you can point to a thousand different things that could have happened, that might have influenced the situation one way or the other. But the reality is that here you had a little boy who was scared. And somehow the idea came to him to focus on his breathing. That's what they tell you in every yoga class—that's what they tell you on every meditation CD I've ever heard. Focus on your breathing. Because when you get into a stressful situation, the natural instinct of the body is to freeze, to stop breathing. It must be a survival mechanism—if they don't hear you breathe, they can't find you. I guess that's the initial form of self-protection."

David considered what Jennifer was saying.

"So he just focused on his breathing, and then

because he's a kid, he realized he had to go to the bathroom?"

"That's about it," Jennifer said. "I know it sounds kind of crazy."

"It's not that it sounds crazy," David said. "It's what we call a movie moment. It's a moment that's so dramatic and remarkable that if it happened in a movie, you'd say, 'That's so cool.' But if somebody told you it happened in real life, you'd say, 'No, that couldn't happen.' It's just a funny thing about the movies—we're willing to give more credibility to what could happen in the story than what did or did not happen in real life."

"I never thought about it that way," Jennifer said. "I just thought it was pretty cool that Austin was able to, I don't know, allow himself to calm down. It makes sense, though. The air that you breathe in really is cooler than the air that you breathe out."

"I just had a thought," David said. "Everybody's always talking about living in the future or in the past, instead of being in the moment. But you know what's funny? You can only breathe...in the present moment. If you're aware of your breathing, you have to be in the moment."

Jennifer considered his words. "It's funny," she said. "Whenever I notice my breathing, it's almost always really shallow. Like I'm afraid something bad is going to happen, and I'm just protecting myself so that no one can hear me breathing. What's that about?"

David nodded. "It's like driving in L.A.," he said, smiling. "You're not practicing defensive driving. You're practicing offensive driving. And if you're breathing at all, you're trying to control yourself from shouting at the other guy or flipping him the bird."

"Not exactly meditative," David admitted. "Not that I'm especially meditative. I keep making my mind up to meditate, and then I keep letting other things get in the way."

"Like what?"

"Like life," David said. "But sometimes I can just sit there for a couple of minutes, especially when I'm stuck in traffic on the 101—don't even ask about traffic on the 101 after, say, three p.m. You move so slowly that I end up doing some of my best meditating then. Mostly about when I'm ever gonna leave L.A."

Jennifer laughed.

"The only time I meditate with any consistency," David continued, grinning, "is when I'm actually sitting in traffic and I'm actually aware of my breathing—not controlling or manipulating it. I actually find myself returning to the present moment. I feel, you know, a sense of peace. Of calm. I'm not worried about the past or the future or when I'm gonna get where I'm going, or what that producer's doing with my screenplay, or what that actor should have done with the lines I wrote. Instead...I'm just...in the flow."

"In the flow of traffic?" Jennifer asked, teasing him again.

"Yeah, in the flow of traffic," David said, with a rueful smile. "In the flow of life. It's about the breathing, but it's really not about the breathing. It's about being present, in the present moment, right here, right now, instead of being a million miles away. Breathing seems to be a ticket to experiencing being in the present."

"Sounds like that's the only ticket you can get on the 101," Jennifer said, laughing. "No speeding tickets there."

"Maybe a ticket for double-parking," David said. "I think you understand what I'm trying to say. Let me try it right now. Without being behind the wheel."

He carefully set his wine glass down on the blanket and closed his eyes.

"I'm going to breathe in now," he said.

David took a long, slow, deep breath. When he had breathed in all he could, he made a little circling motion with his left index finger, and began slowly to exhale out his nose.

Jennifer watched intently.

"It's true," David said, surprised and pleased with his discovery. "The air was cooler going in and warmer going out. Your student was right." He shook his head, amazed at how much more centered he felt after just taking a deep breath. "I guess that's meditation," David said. "I guess you could say he was meditating."

Jennifer nodded slowly as the idea sank in. "You know, I think you're right. I wouldn't say he was conscious of the fact that he was meditating, or that he could possibly use a word like that to label his experience that way. But there's no doubt that what he was doing was calming his mind through meditation, which is I guess something people have been doing for centuries."

"I guess I understand a little more about why you like to teach kids," David said, nodding in approval. "They really can surprise you. The fact that a five-year-old in your class discovered a way to meditate might have saved lives."

Jennifer let the idea sink in. "It really is kind of amazing," Jennifer agreed. "And all he did was think about his breath! It seems so obvious, but I've never even thought to try it."

And then she remembered driving home from school just an hour or two earlier. When she had focused on her breathing, there had been a definite shift in her awareness. It was like she'd been able to tap into the same force that guided her when Bob walked into the classroom with a loaded gun. Maybe being aware of your breathing is the key, she thought with a little twinge of excitement. Maybe that's how you restore that incredible feeling of being aligned with something beyond yourself!

"I want to try it," she announced to David with a newfound sense of determination. "I want to try doing just that: breathing in and breathing out."

He nodded. "We could do it together, right now," he said shyly. "I mean, if you want to. I always tried to center myself before I went out shooting video when I was in the war zones. But I could never sit still long enough. Maybe I just never had a meditation technique I connected with. What if we just took ten breaths right now, and notice the air being cooler going in and warmer going out?"

For a second, David and Jennifer looked awk-wardly at one another, as if the whole thing were somewhat ridiculous—two relative strangers having a picnic dinner, and interrupting it to breathe in and out. Well, Jennifer decided, she had been on stranger dates than this. Although this was not a date, of course. And besides—this was something she really wanted to do. She decided to take the plunge.

"Okay," she said. "Let's do it." She put her wine glass down on the picnic blanket, closed her eyes, and inhaled slowly and deeply. David followed suit.

As she took the first breath, Jennifer felt a sense of anxiousness as she drew cool air into her nostril. There she was, sitting with a guy she'd only just met, trying to meditate in the middle of a park. It was crazy, right? At the thought of the word "crazy," an image of Bob holding the gun flashed across her mind. Then she saw Austin's face and the fear behind it. She felt herself shudder involuntarily as a depth of feeling welled up behind her eyes.

But as she let the breath out, she made a choice. She acknowledged the moment, but then she just…let it be. The feelings of fear and frustration and anxiety crumbled, cracked, and melted away as she focused on the warmth of the air. She felt a head rush that made her almost dizzy. So I can do it, she thought. She embarked on the second breath with a sense of having tasted something delicious.

Meanwhile, David was having a similar experience, though he was taking a different path to get there. As he inhaled, he found himself unable to focus on the coolness of the air. Even though his eyes were closed, his mind began to play a steady stream of images—Jennifer sitting in front of him, the vibrant green of the grass, the impressive size of the oak tree towering above them. When he exhaled, he had completely forgotten about the warmth of the air. Instead he found himself thinking in camera angles and shots, consumed with ideas of how to capture the moment and translate it into film.

For a split second, he opened his eyes to take in more of the beauty. And then he saw Jennifer, sitting just a few inches away from him with her eyes closed, breathing in and breathing out. The sun was reflecting off of her hair like light on a lake. In that moment, he thought that she not only looked unspeakably lovely, but completely and entirely at peace. There was a look of such evident bliss on her face that for a second he was almost jealous. But then he felt a very different emotion, one that startled him in its intensity.

He wanted to reach out and touch her. Ever so gently, not wanting to disturb her meditation, he reached out and laid a hand on top of hers. He felt a warmth and an energy that captivated him. He closed his eyes and fell in sync with her breathing, and an overwhelming sense of calm came over him. David suddenly realized that the stream of mental images had ceased, like someone had pulled a curtain over the stage.

But the moment David reached out and put his hand on Jennifer's, she was jolted back into the land of thought. A hundred different and conflicting thoughts arrived one after another, relentlessly bombarding the very brain that had been so quiet a few moments before. He's touching my hand, she thought. What does it mean that he's touching my hand? Does this mean we are on a date? And is that okay? Once again, Jennifer felt like she was swimming upstream amidst a sea of stressful ruminations. How strange that I can get in the flow when I'm alone, she thought, but the moment someone else comes on the scene, it gets a whole lot harder.

By the end of the ten breaths, Jennifer felt a little drained. David, on the other hand, felt rejuvenated. They opened their eyes at the same moment and smiled at each other.

"That was good," he said, gently releasing her hand. "I feel…refreshed. And I don't think it's the wine."

Jennifer grinned. "I'm not sure if you're supposed to meditate while you're drinking wine," she teased, "or vice versa. But I guess it couldn't hurt this one time."

"I won't tell anybody if you won't," David said with a wink.

At the softness of his gaze, Jennifer forgave herself her inability to meditate.

It's okay, she realized. Everything's going to be okay. You'll get back to that place again. And you know what? Maybe it won't have to be alone.

She couldn't help smiling as both she and David delved hungrily into their lasagna.

Chapter 8

Over their impromptu dinner in the park, David and Jennifer laughed, shared stories about their lives, and talked more about the funny things kindergarteners say. For a while, Jennifer forgot all about the strange circumstances that had brought them together in the first place. But they made their way back to the subject eventually, and David posed a question.

"We've talked a lot about the state of mind of Austin while you were going through that ordeal with the homeless guy," he said, forking a scrumptious piece of lasagna into his mouth. "But what about your state of mind? What were you thinking about? I'm sure this is something that everybody watching the movie will want to know."

For a moment, Jennifer was startled to realize again that people would be watching a movie about her. It was too weird to contemplate, so she set the thought deliberately aside and instead focused on the question.

"To tell you the truth, I've been going over this in my own mind ever since the incident happened," she said. "Even when I'm supposed to be focused on my students, I just keep coming back to that same question. What was I thinking?"

David waited.

"And as best as I can tell, after I realized he had a gun, I wasn't thinking anything at all. I was just... there. I wasn't really thinking about anything. I wasn't thinking, 'Oh my God, he's got a gun, there could be a shooting.' I wasn't going back in my mind to thoughts about school shootings I'd heard of, or putting on the TV and seeing stretchers, or anything horrible like that. I wasn't in the past, going back over events. I wasn't in the future, thinking about consequences. I was just...there."

"Keep going," David said quietly. "This is fascinating."

"Fascinating sounds a little strong," Jennifer said, her tone self-deprecating. "But I'll admit that it's interesting to me. I mean, it really was the most dramatic thing I've ever been through. Or ever hope to go through, for that matter!

"But anyway, I just felt something inside me shift. I wasn't conscious of my breathing, and I don't know if that's something to be ashamed to admit. But I wasn't." Jennifer pondered this statement for a moment to make sure it was accurate. After all, being conscious of her breathing had now brought her back to that same place of non-thought—twice. But had she been thinking about her breathing when she moved into action in the classroom? No, she hadn't. She was sure of it.

"I wasn't conscious of anything," she repeated with confidence. "In my mind, I just transformed the situation from something dangerous into something peaceful." A new thought suddenly struck Jennifer. Maybe it's not the breath, she realized with growing amazement. Maybe the breathing is just one way to access the feeling. A way to kind of…open the door.

David was watching Jennifer as she silently contemplated just as carefully as he was listening to her words. He realized that Jennifer was likely coming to an understanding of her state of mind during the brief ordeal for the very first time—that she was putting words to an experience in a way that she had not done prior to this moment. He watched and listened intently.

Jennifer shook her head. "I don't know if this is going to make any sense," she said.

"I don't think you have to judge what you're thinking about," David told her gently. "Just tell me more."

Jennifer glanced at David, almost to see if she could really trust him with her innermost experience of the event. He is paying me for this, she decided, and the kids are getting the money. She willed herself to go deeper.

"I would really use the word...allow to explain what happened," she said. "I just allowed the situation to unfold. I didn't try to control it. I mean, you only have to control things when you're afraid that you're not going to get an outcome you want, right? And I just sort of envisioned this—I know this is going to sound so wacky and New Age—but I just envisioned this bubble of safety and serenity surrounding my kids. I knew nothing bad was going to happen."

"Like...white light?" David asked, trying to make more specific sense of her experience.

Jennifer bit her lip. "I really wouldn't know how to categorize it in words," she admitted. "I hate to disappoint you," she added sincerely.

"You're not disappointing me," David said, putting his hand up. "This is perfect. Just keep going. Let me not try to put words in your mouth. Bad habit, I guess."

Jennifer grinned. "I guess I do the same thing," she said, then she grew serious again.

"I just knew that everything was fine, and that everything would be fine. I even got the idea in my head that he had a starter's pistol or a cap gun. Later on, the police chief told me it was a loaded .45. Which really floored me. I don't know how I somehow shielded myself from that information. I mean, I don't know much about guns, but I know the difference between a cap pistol and a loaded weapon. Or at least I think I do."

Jennifer sighed, willing herself back into the moment in the classroom, not desiring to relive it but knowing she had to, because of the commitment she had made.

"As I said, I just allowed the situation to unfold. This may sound crazy, because I know that all the reporters were shouting, 'What were you thinking?' But the thing is, I wasn't thinking. I was just allowing. I was just...somehow removed from my normal, thinking self. I mean, I'm the most logical person you ever met. I've got to-do lists up the wazoo. I think through everything before I say it or do it. I never go into class without a lesson plan. I never try to wing it if I had a big weekend and I didn't get a chance to prepare things. I've got my lesson plans prepared weeks—sometimes months in advance. I think through everything."

"And where has that gotten you?" David asked.

Jennifer shrugged. "It's gotten me a great career as a kindergarten teacher, and all the lesson plans anybody could dream of. But that's about it." She paused.

"I think I think too much," she admitted, in a softer voice. She took a sip of wine. "I think I'm addicted to thinking! I think through everything. I meet a guy, and I start thinking about where it's going to go, then I start thinking about where it could go, which is not always positive, and I think about how things could go wrong..." She trailed off, remembering the warmth of David's hand on her own hand when they had breathed together. She'd already started to over-think things with David, she realized with some embarrassment. And she didn't even know if he thought of her as anything but material for a TV movie! Maybe that's just what they did in Hollywood when they meditated—held hands.

"Anyway," she continued, trying not to blush. "I just talk myself out of everything."

David waited, sipping from his glass. He didn't want to interrupt her flow.

"I think," Jennifer began, and then she laughed. "There I go again! I'm thinking again! What I'm try-ing to say is that I think I've thought myself out of just about everything that I really want to have in life. Except for the career. That I've got nailed down. But I'm twenty-nine—and I know people are getting mar-ried later and all that. But I never thought I would. I'm kind of traditional that way. Coming from Hollywood, you must think I'm some kind of freak."

David quickly shook his head.

"Exactly the opposite," David said. "Listening to you, I realize what a freak show I'm caught up in. You can take my word for that."

"I suppose," Jennifer said. "But it's like, for that one moment, everything else just faded away. No thoughts, no worries, no fear. Just complete and total peace. I was just…present in the moment. If that doesn't sound freaky, I don't know what does." She took another sip of wine and giggled. "You know what's really crazy? I don't even know how long it lasted. Was the guy in my room three minutes? Five minutes? Half an hour? I have no idea."

"About twenty-five minutes," David said. "Long enough for a rousing chorus of Barney, according to The New York Times."

Jennifer cocked her head, and then remembered singing Barney with the stranger the way she might suddenly, in the middle of the day, remember a piece of a dream from the night before.

She grinned. "He sang along," she said. "That was very sweet when he did that. A homeless guy with a loaded .45, singing the Barney song!"

"That's a movie moment, too," David said, smiling back at her.

"I'll tell you what's going on for me," Jennifer said. "I feel like I'm in a therapy session. But what's happening is that I'm realizing right now that this might have been the first time in my adult life—or maybe in my whole life since I was my students' age—that I wasn't thinking."

"Which means what exactly?" David asked, studying her.

Jennifer took her time before she answered, and when she spoke, she spoke slowly. "It's as if…the part of my brain that's addicted to thinking and thinking and thinking, and generating all kinds of thought, most of it useless, this endless stream of chatter—it's like it finally got silenced. For the first time ever. And I was able to reflect back and realize I was not thinking.

"My mind was at peace. I didn't make a conscious decision. I didn't think my way through it. I didn't make a to-do list of how I would make a semicircle and have the kids sing songs and get the gun away from the guy somehow. I just was. I just…allowed. It's like…I got quiet inside. And I made the right choices, and everything worked out fine."

Jennifer fell silent, looking intently at David, feeling exposed. Did he think she was crazy? Just some ditzy schoolteacher, who was starting to sound like a guy you'd hear on late night TV pitching a meditation CD?

"Would you allow me to kiss you?" David asked quietly.

Startled, Jennifer found herself slipping back into her normal mode of thinking, brain chatter, and control. But then, something shifted. She allowed herself to slip into the same peaceful state of mind that she had first experienced in her classroom when the stranger arrived, and again in her car driving home, and, most recently, sitting with David as she felt the coolness and warmth of her breath. This time, she didn't do anything. She merely…allowed.

"I would allow that," she said simply.

David reached over, stroked her hair, and kissed her gently on the lips.

When they disengaged, Jennifer looked at him with mild surprise. She was at a loss for words—a situation in which she rarely found herself. As a teacher who was accustomed to curious kindergartners asking her a thousand questions each day, Jennifer always had an answer for everything. But now, as she stared at David, she was speechless. A feeling of bliss washed over her like a cool spring rain, and like someone wandering through the desert, she drank it up.

Then, very slowly, and still savoring the feeling of David's lips on hers, she pulled herself reluctantly from the moment and re-emerged into reality. She noticed that the last rays of sunshine were seeping through the oak leaves and falling onto her shoulders. Her skin felt warm.

"I didn't know that was in the script," she said coyly, referring to the kiss.

David looked surprised by his own actions. And in fact, he was. In the waning sunlight, there was a charming flush to Jennifer's cheeks and an illuminating candor in her eyes that he hadn't been prepared for. He'd been completely smitten when he asked if he could kiss her. And when his lips brushed hers, he felt as if he had brushed up against something he had never before experienced in his life. All of this was surprising.

So perhaps it wasn't at all surprising that he wanted to kiss her again.

"I guess it's in the script now," he said softly, leaning closer to Jennifer's radiant face.

"It is now," she agreed, and they kissed again.

Chapter 9

"That kiss definitely wasn't in the script," David said, looking pleased and sheepish at the same time.

"I just... allowed it," Jennifer said.

But suddenly, a hundred different thoughts rushed into her head at once. She felt off-balance and defensive. "Is that part of the deal?" she asked, surprised by her own sharpness. "Is that... something that you do with everybody you write about?"

David looked stricken. "I've never done that before in my life," he said, the words tumbling out of his mouth. "I swear. I— It's a line I've never crossed before. Even a little kiss like that."

Jennifer studied him. She took a slow breath in and out, and decided that he was telling the truth.

"I guess you just allowed it to happen, too," she said, wanting to believe that this was the truth.

David, embarrassed, looked her in the eye.

"Pretty much," he said.

"So that's what you call a little kiss in Hollywood?" Jennifer asked, a playful glint in her eye.

"I guess," David said, not sure where she was going.

"Well, then," Jennifer purred, feeling a little more confident. "What does a big one look like?"

David grinned, leaned forward, and this time their lips met in a long embrace. For several glorious seconds, they were both able to let go of all the thoughts and concerns swirling around in their heads and allow themselves to be exactly as they were: two people, under an oak tree in the middle of a park, kissing.

When they finally pulled apart, they stared at one another for a long time.

"You're different from the women I meet in Hollywood," David said finally. "You're a real human being."

"You're different from the men I've been dating

for the last three years," Jennifer admitted. "That's because there haven't been any."

David shook his head in a gently reproaching way. "You've got to get out more often," he said.

"I'd like to," Jennifer admitted. "But there's always a lesson plan or something that has to be taken care of."

"How about taking care of Jennifer?" David asked, sipping his wine again. "You're out there taking care of your kids, and I'm sure your home is absolutely immaculate. And your IRA is in order, and I'm sure you floss after every meal. But what about the person underneath all that?"

Jennifer shrugged. "Nobody home," she said. And then she added, "That's not fair. That's not fair to me. Somebody's home. It's just that I haven't gone to see her very often."

David nodded.

"What is Jennifer like?" he asked. "Not, what does Jennifer have to do, because it's the right thing to do, because it's going to take care of her students, or because it matches the drapes."

"I don't have drapes," Jennifer said, grinning.

"You know what I mean," David said. "What does

Jennifer like to do that she doesn't normally get to do? Because she just never lets herself go do it?"

Jennifer thought for a long time before she answered.

"I'm drawing a blank," she said. "You must think I'm a real idiot."

David shook his head slowly. "I think you're the most wonderful woman I've ever met," he said. "And that's not just Hollywood talk. That's just how I feel."

Jennifer looked at him as if he were feeding her some sort of line, or more accurately, as if she hoped he wasn't feeding her some sort of line.

"I'm not joking," David said, and his tone indicated to Jennifer that he was telling the truth.

"You're smart as hell, and you could have done anything you wanted in the business world and you'd have made a fortune by now. I saw what kind of negotiator you are when you got the two million for the kids! But you became a kindergarten teacher because you love children. You're acting on your beliefs. On your character. Everybody says they want to do that, but very few people do."

David's earnest admiration tumbled out like a pent-up river once the dam has broken. "You're an amazingly resourceful person," he went on. "I just can't get over what you did or how you did it. I'm still trying to understand this whole thing of how you allowed it to happen instead of how you made something happen. I kept putting myself in your shoes, and I would have ended up forcing some sort of horrible confrontation with that guy. I'm sure something bad would have happened."

"Don't say that," Jennifer said quietly. "You never know how you'll rise to an occasion until you actually get there."

David shrugged. "I suppose," he said. "But on top of that, you're a very warm, beautiful, giving person, and for whatever reason, I don't know if you got hurt in your last relationship or what, but you just haven't had the opportunity to nurture someone else, or yourself, for that matter."

"Is that going to end up in your portrait of me for the movie?" Jennifer asked.

"Only if you want it to," David said. "We can make the character any way we like. If there are parts of your story you don't want in there, just say so. The last thing I would do is embarrass you."

Jennifer blushed and looked down at her hands.

"So you're not going to talk about how I've spent the last three years lurking on online dating sites?"

David grinned. "I think that'll be our little secret," he said. "Seriously, what does Jennifer like to do… for Jennifer? And I don't mean crossing another item off your to-do list, whether it's a lesson plan or going to the gym or, I don't know, getting some touch-up paint and taking care of that scratch on your Prius."

"How did you know I drive a Prius?" she asked.

"Lucky guess," David said, his grin widening. "Seriously, what do you like to do that never makes your to-do list?"

Jennifer thought for a long time. Again, nothing came to mind. And then she decided that instead of trying to force an answer, which didn't seem to be coming, even to a question seemingly as simple as the one David had posed, she decided she would allow an answer to come.

"I like to laugh," she blurted out.

David looked pleased. "Perfect," he said. "I was reading the local paper this morning—I had a lot of time on my hands, while you were at school—and I saw that there's a comedy club in town. Do you want to go?"

"Sure," Jennifer said. "But when? I mean, you're only going to be here for a couple more nights. Do we have to make, I don't know, reservations?"

"What's that line from a Tom Cruise movie?" David asked. "Didn't he say something like 'There's a time and a place for spontaneity'?"

Jennifer stared at him. "What do you mean, you want to go tonight?" she asked. "But it's a school night!"

David shook his head and laughed. "People can have fun on school nights," he said. "And besides, the show's at 7:30. I can have you home by 9:15, and you can be in bed by 9:30."

"Is this something for the movie?" Jennifer asked, suddenly feeling cautious.

David shook his head.

"It's for Jennifer," he said. "Jennifer's been through a lot. Jennifer needs to laugh."

Jennifer pondered this statement and nodded.

"Jennifer does need to laugh," she said. "Jennifer hasn't had a good laugh in a long time. Let's do it." She jumped up and stretched.

David checked his watch. "No need to rush—we have time," he said.

"You think?" Jennifer asked, reaching in her purse and checking her cell phone for the time.

"The show isn't until 7:30," David said, "and it's 6:45 now. And unless I've really messed up my directions, the comedy club is less than fifteen minutes from where we are right now. In fact, I think everything in Greenfield is less than fifteen minutes from where we are right now."

"Don't go ragging on Greenfield," Jennifer said. "It's a pretty great place to live."

"It doesn't have as many bars open 'til four in the morning as my neighborhood in Hollywood," David said. "But on the other hand, it is a lot easier to find a parking space."

"One of our many civic virtues," Jennifer said, smiling. "Let's clean up our picnic and get there early. I want to sit down front, so the comedians can make fun of us. Well, not me. Just you."

"What are they going to make fun of me for?" David asked, surprised.

"I don't know," Jennifer said, a twinkle in her eye. "I'm sure they'll think of something. Come on, let's eat."

Chapter 10

Two hours later, Jennifer and David were sitting at a table just a few feet away from the stage at the Greenfield Laugh Emporium, the local comedy club. Ron Kenney, the comedian, was halfway through his routine.

"You know, nowadays," Kenney was saying into the microphone, "everything's all about do-it-yourself. We're living in a do-it-yourself society— we've got do-it-yourself books, do-it-yourself video games, do-it-yourself websites. Hell, I even live in a do-it-yourself household. The three words I hear from my wife on a daily basis? I'll give you a hint: they're not 'I love you.'"

The audience at the club chuckled appreciatively.

"Back in the old days," Kenney went on, "a fifteen-year-old kid got paid to bag up my groceries. But the other day I go to the neighborhood grocery store to do a little shopping, and now even the check-out line is do-it-yourself. You put your stuff on the belt and there's an automated attendant who actually wants to communicate with you. She's a woman, of course."

The audience groaned.

"So I'm putting my groceries on the belt, and I get to the fresh produce. And turns out you can't just swipe the produce and go—you have to key in the product numbers for your fruits and veggies. So I key in the product number for my kiwis.

"'Please place your kiwis on the belt,' the woman says, like she knows me and my kiwis personally. So I put my kiwis on the belt. After all, I'm not trying to upset the flow of things.

"So then I key in the product number for my cantaloupes. Who doesn't love a good cantaloupe? Best breakfast fruit ever invented.

"'How many melons do you have?' the woman asks.

"'This woman's getting a little familiar. But

there's a man behind me with a cluster of bananas who's looking kind of antsy. So I key in quantity, two. Two melons.

"'Please place your melons on the belt,' the woman says. So that's exactly where I place my melons. On the belt. And I'm trying to be cool about it.

"Then I pull out the bag of almonds I got from the dried goods aisle, 'cuz my wife is crazy about almonds. I key in the number.

"'How many nuts do you have?' the woman prods. 'Please place your nuts on the belt.'

"And I want to say, 'Gettin' a little fresh for Aisle 11, don't you think?'"

Gales of appreciative laughter filled the club.

"The perils of modern day grocery stores, ladies and gentlemen," Kenney said with a grin. "Beware of your fruits and nuts."

The lights in the club were dim, but Jennifer could see David's laughing face in the soft light of a tea candle on the center of their table. She was drinking the sweetest mojito she had ever tasted. It suddenly occurred to her that she was having more fun than she had had in years.

She leaned close to David and whispered, "I can't believe this many people come out on a Wednesday night."

He smiled. "Not everybody has to get up early to teach kindergarten tomorrow," he said. "And even people with jobs like to get out once in a while."

"You don't have a job," Jennifer said, a tinge of admiration in her voice.

"You're my job," David said, and they turned their attention back to the comedian.

Kenney was winding down. "One more thing, ladies and gentlemen," Kenney was saying. "All kidding aside, it's not every day that you're in the presence of true heroism. I know she's going to be surprised to hear me say this, but sitting right close to the stage is the brave young woman who saved the lives of all those kindergarten students, Jennifer Albright. Jennifer, take a bow."

Jennifer, flushed with embarrassment, blinked as one of the stagehands trained a spotlight on her face, and the audience burst into prolonged applause.

"Did you tell him I was here?" Jennifer whispered uncomfortably to David as the applause continued.

He shook his head quickly. "Of course not. It's not like I'd need to," he added. "You're pretty recognizable. And it was your idea to sit down front."

"I guess you're right," Jennifer said, forcing a smile and waving to the crowd. She then glanced up at the comedian as if to say, enough already.

"You've been a great audience," Kenney said. "And let Jennifer Albright be an inspiration to you. Good night!"

Kenney took his bows and waved good night to the crowd.

The lights came on in the club, and David and Jennifer stood to leave.

"That took me by surprise," Jennifer said.

"I'll bet it did," David said. "You'd better get used to that, though. I think you're going to be America's sweetheart for a long time."

"As long as I'm your sweetheart," Jennifer murmured, not quite loud enough for David to hear.

"What?" David asked. "It's a little loud in here."

"Nothing," Jennifer said, surprising herself by what she had blurted out. "Anyway, this was a really great idea. I haven't laughed like that for I don't know how long."

"Those guys were really funny," David said. "It's a gift to get up there and make people laugh."

Since they were at the front of the packed showroom, getting out was not going to be a quick proposition.

"We might as well sit down again for a minute and let this place clear out," David said.

"We could do that," Jennifer said.

They watched the crowd leave. "It is kind of amazing," Jennifer said. "All these people out on a weeknight."

"And some of them really do have jobs," David said. "I would venture to say just about all of them."

Jennifer shook her head. "It's really amazing how you can just get so caught up in your routines that you never break out and do anything fun. I'll bet you're always doing incredibly fun things all the time."

David rolled his eyes. "Oh, it's so glamorous. Hanging out with movie stars. Going to the Oscars. It's incredible that anybody gets any work done."

"You've been to the Oscars?" Jennifer asked, amazed.

David made a face as if to say, it's not that big a deal.

"It's actually the most boring thing you can imagine," he said. "The show goes on for four and a half hours, and you don't even see the big stars most of the time. They're not sitting through the whole thing. They're off in rooms on the side, waiting until their nominations are called. It's not exactly a night of fun. Especially if you've been nominated for anything."

"Have you?" Jennifer asked, a newfound level of respect in her voice.

"Once," David said. "Didn't win, though. No big deal."

"Still," Jennifer said. "To be nominated for an Oscar—that's pretty amazing."

"It definitely helped my visibility," David said. "Otherwise, I probably wouldn't have been in a position to make the deal you and I made for this movie. So in that sense, I guess it's a good thing.

"But seriously, it's not like I have some sort of incredibly glamorous lifestyle. I live in a two-bedroom apartment in Hollywood. The actual Hollywood, the one where drug addicts and runaways live. Not the one they talk about on the Oscars. I use the second bedroom as my writing room, and there are some days I don't get out of my place until about four or five in the afternoon. I hang out with my friends, but it's not like I'm hitting any Hollywood parties or going to bars until four in the morning. You can't really do that stuff and get your work done."

"You're kind of like me," Jennifer said.

"Well, not quite," David admitted, a sly grin crossing his face. "I don't make my bed every day, and I'm guessing you do. I'm sure you don't consider Pop Tarts a food group. And your favorite restaurant in the whole world probably isn't a hamburger stand that hasn't changed its menu in sixty years."

Jennifer was vaguely aware that the crowd had thinned out, but she and David stayed seated at the front table. She was surprised to find that she wasn't even concerned about the time. She never went out on a school night...usually she'd be getting into her pajamas and crawling into bed within the hour. But now she was totally breaking her normal routine and having a blast. And she didn't feel tired in the slightest. On the contrary: she was engaged in conversation with David and energized from the comedy show. She actually felt physically lighter from an hour and a half of belly laughs. She couldn't remember the last time she'd laughed so hard.

"Well, you may be right about the bed and the Pop Tarts," she said to David, giving him a wry look. "But I love hamburgers. I'd love to go to a hamburger place that hasn't changed its menu in sixty years." Then she paused and let out a sly laugh. "Wait a minute. You're not talking about McDonald's, are you?"

David shook his head. "It's called The Apple Pan," he said. "And they have really awesome pie."

"I can't remember the last time I had a slice of pie," Jennifer admitted. "There's a place not too far from here that makes really great apple pie. Shall we get some?"

David narrowed his eyes. "You're the one who has to be in bed at 9:30," David said, teasing her. "I wouldn't want to be responsible for breaking your perfect record."

Jennifer nudged him on the shoulder. "Why don't you leave the comedy to the professionals," she said, pointing to the stage, teasing him right back. "I think one night won't kill me."

"Only if it'll add some details to the story I'm going to write about your life," David said. "Otherwise, I'm dropping you off at your place right now."

"I think everything you need to know about me, you can learn at Ellen's Pie Shop," Jennifer said, giving him a broad smile. "Come on, let's get out of here."

And they did.

Chapter 11

Twenty minutes later, Jennifer and David were digging into the largest slices of apple pie David had ever seen. The pie was warm, garnished with a generous scoop of vanilla ice cream, and a slice of cheese. Alongside were cups of steaming black coffee.

"I'm gonna guess," David said, his mouth full, "that this is the first time you've allowed yourself to eat pie in five years."

Jennifer giggled. "You're not so far from the truth," she said. "I guess I'm pretty rigorous about my diet."

"You gotta lighten up," David said, teasing her.

"I'm afraid that if I lighten up, that's when I'll get really heavy."

"One piece of pie won't kill you," David said.

"I suppose not," Jennifer said.

The pie shop, another family owned institution in Greenfield, famous for its burgers and tuna salad sandwiches in addition to its freshly baked pies, was fairly empty. Jennifer and David were sitting at the window, watching the darkened street through red checked curtains. At the counter, the shop owner, an old man with a round belly and kind face, was counting down the register. It was, after all, almost ten o'clock on a weeknight, and the good citizens of Greenfield who had ventured out for entertainment or shopping by now had returned to their homes to prepare for a night of sleep and another day of work. Not Jennifer and David; they were doing all the wildest things you could do in Greenfield, which pretty much consisted of going to a comedy club and then topping it off with some apple pie.

"I'll tell you something crazy," Jennifer said. "I don't wear a watch, and not just because I can tell the time on my cell phone. It's because I can tell you instinctively what time it is, practically to the minute, anytime of the night or day. It's like I'm totally attuned to what time it is."

David blinked at her. He raised one eyebrow and nodded slowly, looking fairly impressed.

"How come?" he said, helping himself to another big bite of apple pie. Then, as an afterthought, he added, "I've never seen pie served with cheese before. I guess it's some kind of tradition."

Jennifer took a small spoonful of ice cream and held it in the air, considering it before she put it in her mouth.

"I just feel like I've always got to be on time for everything," she said. "So my whole body is attuned to what time it is. That way, if I'm teaching, I know how much time there is left in a class but without having to turn around and look at the clock. If I'm at the gym, I know how far along I am in my workout before I have to stop and get ready for dinner. And at night, I know what time it is when I'm on the computer, before I have to look at the little time box or whatever you call it and shut it down to go to bed."

"What are you doing on the computer?" David asked, teasing her again. "Lurking for men you're not going to talk to?"

Jennifer gave him a sidelong glance.

"Guilty," she said. "I guess it's just safer that way. And it's safe with you, because you're leaving town in a couple of days. Even though I let you kiss me."

"Yeah, you allowed that."

"But when I'm with you," Jennifer said, returning to her main point, "…and I can say this again because I know you're leaving and I'll never see you again, so it doesn't matter what I say…"

David stirred at those words, glancing at her, but not saying anything.

"…it just feels like time is standing still," Jennifer finished. "I've really forgotten what it's like to have fun. And when you're enjoying yourself, time stands still."

"A lot of cultures say there's no such thing as time," David said. "You go to a lot of places in the world, they don't believe time exists. To the extent that they've even heard of time, they believe it's something that our culture has invented, in order to make ourselves crazy, and everybody else, too. Time is an illusion."

Jennifer took a small bite of apple pie and looked out the plate glass windows of the pie shop, considering David's words.

"Well, getting to work on time isn't an illusion," Jennifer countered.

David grinned. "There you go, going all rational on me again. No, being late for work isn't an illusion. But who invented work, anyway?"

Jennifer shook her head. "This is getting a little too philosophical for me," she said. "I'm happier when I can deal with real things."

"Like the way I feel about you?" David asked quietly.

His words took Jennifer aback.

"What?" she asked, not knowing what else to say.

"Uh, nothing," David said, reddening. "It just slipped out."

Jennifer studied him. Even though it had been three full years since her last relationship had ended, and none too happily, she was sure the last thing she needed in life was another man somehow making fun of her or taking her feelings lightly.

"Did you mean what you said?" she asked.

David nodded slowly. He put his spoon down. "I'm sorry I'm only here for a few days," he said.

"It isn't as glamorous as Hollywood," Jennifer said, testing him in an offhand way.

"Glamour isn't everything it's cracked up to be," David replied. And then suddenly, he shifted gears. "Do you like the symphony?"

Jennifer shrugged. "I guess," she said. "I don't know too much about it. Why?"

"Well, in my copious free time this afternoon—" David began.

"Copious," Jennifer said. "Great SAT word."

"I am a writer," David said, giving her a gentle grin. "As I was saying, in my copious spare time, I noticed that the Greenfield Symphony Orchestra has a concert tomorrow night. They're doing Beethoven's 7th and Mozart's 40th. Would that interest you?"

"Beethoven's 7th what?" Jennifer asked innocently.

David's grin widened. "Beethoven's 7th," he explained. "And Mozart's 40th Symphony, the G-minor. Got a thing about classical music. I actually took the liberty of… buying two tickets," he said. He reached into his pocket, pulled them out, and placed them on the counter. Jennifer picked them up and studied them.

"You bought concert tickets?" she asked, surprised.

"It's my last night here in Greenfield," he said. "I figured that by then I'll have gotten everything I needed for the story. So I was thinking that maybe just to... I don't know. Thank you for your time. Celebrate. I don't know what you'd call it. I just thought..."

"I'd love to," Jennifer said happily. "But you're going to have to forgive me. I don't know much about that kind of music. I mean, I took piano lessons when I was a little kid, but I didn't really have the fine motor control, and I got bored and quit after a couple of years."

David gave her his gentle grin. "They won't be looking to you to play anything," he said, the corners of his eyes crinkling. "All we have to do is sit and listen."

Jennifer returned a wry smile. "I think I can do that," she said. "That was really thoughtful of you. Thank you."

"I should be thanking you," David said. "You've given me the story of the century."

"Story of the century?" Jennifer asked. "Girl saves classroom full of little kids?"

David shook his head. "Even better than that," he said quietly, taking her hand. "Boy meets girl."

Jennifer put down her spoon and turned to face him.

"Do you always fall in love with the subjects of your stories?" Jennifer asked, again testing him to see how truthful he was being. There was no room in her heart for further disappointment.

"Let's see," David said, not relinquishing her hand and rubbing his chin with his free hand. "The time I wrote a movie about the man who married a woman with five children because he always wanted a big family—didn't fall in love with him.

"The time I wrote a movie about a woman who weighed 500 pounds and hadn't been outside in six years, and found a doctor who came to her house every day for eighteen months until she got her weight down to 140 pounds—no, I didn't fall in love with her. Although I bet she really liked apple pie."

Jennifer laughed.

David shook his head. "It's never happened before," he admitted quietly.

"Is it happening now?" Jennifer asked softly, touching her hair with her free hand.

"You could say that," David allowed.

"I could say that, too," Jennifer said. "It's just too bad you live so far from here."

"Yeah," David said. "It is."

David, feeling self-conscious by now, let go of her hand and turned his attention back to his coffee and pie. "I bet you don't know what time it is right now," he told Jennifer.

"You're right about that," she said. "I've got no idea. And I don't even care."

Chapter 12

The time could not pass quickly enough for David as he waited for Jennifer's teaching day to come to an end. He had agreed to pick her up from the school, and when sitting around his hotel room had become unbearable, he had taken off to meet her nearly an hour early. He ended up sitting anxiously in his convertible in the school parking lot, the top down once again because it was another perfect spring day. For awhile he busied himself drumming his fingers on the steering wheel, then he turned to flipping absently through the radio stations. Finally he decided to take a stroll down a tree-lined street adjacent to the school.

As he walked, he let himself be lulled into the harmony of nature. Each house seemed to have a garden more beautiful than the last, tidy plots of earth overflowing with marigolds and tulips and daffodils in full bloom. He imagined the lives of the people in every home, and the way in which they tended their particular flowers. In his mind, twin sisters tended a patch of lilies older than themselves, a bachelor planted a tiny evergreen in fresh soil, and a mother who had lost a son watered a solitary rose bush as the sun set.

David smiled as the thoughts wove themselves together in his head to form a kind of narrative of the people of Greenfield. He had lived in a world of images and language for as long as he could remember. Even as a child he loved telling stories as a way to paint pictures. One day, he wrote one of those stories down. The rest, as they say, was history.

Inspired by his experience with Jennifer the day before, David decided to try an experiment. As he walked along the street, soaking up the glorious colors and scents of the flowers, he stopped inventing. For a moment, he stopped constructing histories and stories and lives and images, and just allowed himself to be amidst the flowers. He inhaled and smelled their sweetness. He saw their hues fade into one another as he softened his gaze. He felt a slight breeze ruffle the collar of his shirt.

And in that moment, he felt a kind of blankness, as if his mind—always so full of particular words and phrases for his next screenplay—turned into a blank white screen. It's like he simply stopped thinking. The image bank emptied out, and in its place a profound feeling of happiness spread through David's entire being.

Suddenly, a shrill ring pierced the silence and jolted David out of his reverie. He glanced down at his cell phone. It was his producer.

Slightly annoyed at the interruption, he answered.

For the next five minutes, David listened while his boss yelled into the other end of the line. Tom had clearly been having a bad day and was taking it out on the person who was farthest away. Mostly he was venting about matters completely unrelated to business, but he ended the call by chastising David for not having faxed him notes on "the kindergarten dame"— as he called Jennifer. David tried to point out that his first interview had only been the day before, but Tom would have none of it.

"Get me something, and get it soon," he growled. "And don't think that you're on country time just because you're hanging out with a bunch of hicks. This isn't a vacation. You'll stick to an L.A. schedule no matter where you are, got it?"

"Yes, sir," David said, trying to keep his voice steady.

"Story meeting tomorrow," Tom barked. "We're not cutting you any breaks." And with that, he hung up.

David noticed that his hand was shaking as he put his phone back into his pocket. He was so tired of Tom's mood swings—some days he could be totally charming and act like David's best bud, and other days he was a condescending jerk. All the old frustrations and emotions flared up as David replayed all the unpleasant moments that had passed between them.

But then a strange thing happened. David remembered the very clear experience of being free of thought that he had enjoyed just minutes before the call. How easily he'd allowed himself to be distracted! And how quickly that incredible feeling of peace had disappeared.

And then something even stranger occurred. For the first time, David saw his producer in a different light. He pondered the trouble he knew Tom was having at home, with an absent wife and a daughter who was in and out of the hospital. Then he pondered Tom as a human being with his own set of heartbreaks, griefs, and frustrations.

With this new perspective, David's relationship with his producer seemed less like a challenge, and more like an opportunity for growth. He could visualize Tom as a kind of mirror—a man who, in many ways, revealed a lot of truth to David about his own life. For one thing, David wasn't sure he was happy with his career. He could easily see himself becoming jaded and bitter like Tom in another fifteen years if he stayed on the same path he was on. So maybe it's time I got honest with myself about it, he thought. That also meant getting serious about finding a real place to live, a place he loved and cared for like the people in Greenfield who loved and cared for their gardens with such devotion; a place that could be home. David didn't know if he'd ever find a place like that, but he knew one thing for certain: it certainly wasn't in Hollywood.

The more David viewed Tom as a sounding board, the more his own inner state underwent a complete transformation. Instead of the boiling anger he'd felt just a few moments before, the stream of negative thoughts and emotions was replaced with a sense of gratitude. The insights were coming fast and furious and had completely obliterated the upset. He was almost tempted to text his producer and say, "Thank you for teaching me that about myself!"

But instead, David turned around and began walking back to the school, his peace and happiness intact. He knew he had Jennifer to thank for this. He was discovering something with her that was entirely new for him—a kind of different way of being in the world. And while he wasn't sure exactly what it was or how to describe it, he knew he wanted more.

David was striding up to the school when the bell rang and children came streaming out of the front doors and rushing towards the buses or the curb where their parents waited. David craned his neck, trying to spot Jennifer in the crowd. At last she emerged from the building, looking bright and cheerful in a simple khaki skirt and pastel green cardigan. To David, she was the perfect embodiment of spring.

David was in gym clothes that he had purchased at a local sporting goods store that morning, and Jennifer raised her eyebrows curiously at his outfit.

"Working out?" she asked companionably as she got into his car.

"It's what you'd normally do, right?" David asked. "So I thought maybe you'd want to grab a workout. I don't want your life to be more disrupted than it has to be."

Jennifer just closed her eyes and laughed. "Are you kidding me?" she asked. "Exactly what part of my life hasn't been changed? I have this bizarre situation in my classroom, the international media comes swarming to my town, Hollywood comes calling in the form of you with a check for me and the kids, I'm with a guy I like for the first time in I don't know how long, and you're telling me that you don't want my life to be disrupted? Exactly what part of my life was the way it was?"

David started the engine. "Could we go back to the part about being with a guy you like?" he asked. "Anyway, the guy you like thought that maybe you'd want to go to the gym, since that's what you normally do."

Jennifer thought about it for a moment. "But it's your last day in town," she said. "Don't you want to do something a little more...special?"

"Well," David said, "We do have the concert planned for tonight," he said, brandishing again the pair of tickets he'd bought for the Greenfield Symphony. He handed them to Jennifer for inspection. "But just going to the gym right now would be special enough." He looked sheepish. "I think this is going to sound like I'm a lovesick high school kid, but doing anything with you would be special."

Jennifer studied him, involuntarily going to the place inside of her where she immediately assumed that people were making light of her feelings. Once again, as far as she could tell, David was not.

"There's nothing wrong with being a lovesick high school student," Jennifer said. "The problem comes when people stop feeling that way."

"Makes sense," David said.

Jennifer nodded. "I'd invite you in but... Why don't I invite you in?"

"I thought you'd never ask," David said, grinning. And he drove the short distance back to Jennifer's home.

Once inside, Jennifer went into her bedroom to change while David looked around. The place was certainly different from his home—meticulously arranged, certainly, but also warm, cozy, and inviting. David found himself torn between taking mental notes about the perfectly arrayed spice rack—he glanced and saw that her spices were alphabetized—and feeling a little creepy for violating her privacy. The dual role in which he found himself—TV writer interviewing a subject, and guy interested in a girl—created an uncomfortable conflict in his mind. Well, one more day, he thought, then I can go back and write this thing, and just get it out of my system. And then we'll see where things go from there.

Jennifer emerged in gym clothes—shorts and a T-shirt that accented her athletic figure—and the two of them headed for the gym, once again in David's car, Jennifer offering directions. It wasn't that far—nothing was that far in Greenfield.

"My gym is about two miles from my house," David said as he drove. "To get there, you pass two movie studios, thirty-six 7-Elevens, two Taco Bells, 116 homeless people, and Grauman's Chinese Theater."

"Sounds romantic," Jennifer said.

"I left out all the drug dealers and pickpockets you also pass on the way," David said. "People always find Hollywood to be a little less romantic than they expect."

They pulled up at her gym. With his usual easy smile, David talked his way out of paying for a guest pass, and they headed to the stationary cycles.

"I usually start off with forty-five minutes on the bicycle," Jennifer said, "and then I do some light weights."

"Sounds good to me," David said. "To be honest, I don't even remember the last time I went to the gym."

"You stay in shape," Jennifer said.

"I owe it all to my diet of Velveeta and crackers," David said, grinning. "They're far more nutritious than most people realize."

"I never knew that," Jennifer said, deadpan, and they both cracked up.

They found two side-by-side, vacant bikes, climbed on, and started pedaling. "I've always had this dream," Jennifer said, "of going to Hawaii and doing the Ironman."

David looked at her in surprise. "Are you kidding me? Isn't that like a day-long race?"

Jennifer nodded. "You swim more than two miles," she said, pedaling away on her bike, "and then you bike more than a hundred miles, and then you run a marathon."

"What do you do after that?" David asked. "Wrestle a tiger?"

Jennifer laughed. "No, after the marathon you're done," she said.

"What a relief," David said. "It sounded like you'd be just warming up."

"Whenever I travel," Jennifer said, "I make the trip around a race. I've gone to New York to do the marathon, I've gone to San Diego—hey, your part of the woods, sort of—to do a triathlon, stuff like that. But the Hawaii Ironman is still my dream."

"Sounds like my nightmare," David said. "When I go to Hawaii, I just lie on the beach."

"I've done that," Jennifer said, starting to break a light sweat from her exertions. David was barely turning the pedals. "But I get restless when I'm on a trip. If I don't have it organized around something, I don't know what to think."

"There you go again," David said. "It's the thinking."

Jennifer gave him a blank look.

"Haven't you ever just gone on a vacation and…done nothing?" David asked. "Just not thought at all?"

Jennifer searched her memory.

"There was one time, I guess," she said. "I went with a…friend," she said, not quite sure how to repackage her past for the conversation.

"You went with a boyfriend," David said, filling in the uncomfortable gap. "It's no big deal. So you went with a boyfriend—"

"I don't know why it's so awkward for me to say something like that," Jennifer said, brushing a strand of damp hair off her forehead. "Anyway, he and I went to Jamaica. And it was really just what you said. I guess we just kind of got into the rhythms of the place. We forgot what day it was. We nearly missed our flight home."

"That's what I'm talking about," David said. "No marathons on that trip?"

Jennifer shook her head. "No, we just hung out. We rented motor scooters and went all over the island. People there have such a different sense of time. For somebody like me, it was a real adjustment. At first, I thought, 'Man, these people don't have any sense of time.' Everything was always late. Nothing happened when it was supposed to. It was really frustrating at first. But after a while, I sort of… surrendered to it."

"You allowed it," David said, grinning.

Jennifer nodded. "Exactly," she said, pedaling slightly slower. "I allowed it. I just said to myself, 'This is the way it is down here, so quit fighting it.'"

"And?" David asked.

"And," Jennifer said, remembering back. "I guess it was the best trip I'd ever taken."

"What happened to the guy?" David asked.

Jennifer turned to look at him, trying to decide why he was asking.

"Are you asking for personal or professional reasons?" she asked.

David paused before he spoke. "A little of both," he admitted.

Jennifer gave a small sigh. "That's the guy I mentioned, the relationship that ended three years ago." She lapsed into silence.

David knew better than to interrupt the silence.

Jennifer, pedaling slightly more slowly, glanced at the bank of televisions overhead. They offered the usual babble of news, sports, panel shows, and other forgettable stuff.

"He asked me to marry him," Jennifer said.

"And?" David asked, his voice quiet now. It seemed strange to him that another man would have asked

Jennifer to marry him, but it seemed even stranger to him that he would care.

"I told him I'd think about it," Jennifer said, wincing at the painful memory. "And that's exactly what I did. I thought about it from every conceivable angle and possibility. I studied it and studied it and studied it, and thought and thought and thought. And I thought about it for months. And by the time I thought that the answer should be yes, his feelings were so hurt that I couldn't make my mind up sooner that he moved on." Jennifer looked at the gym floor, barely paying attention to the fact that her legs were hardly moving at all.

"And that was three years ago," she said. "I feel like my habit of compulsive thinking cost me a relationship. A marriage. It's all I've thought about for the last three years."

For his part, David felt overjoyed that she had turned down the proposal.

"There must have been some other reason," he said. "Maybe you weren't ready, or he really wasn't the right guy, or something else wasn't right."

Jennifer shook her head sadly. "I've thought about that, too," she admitted in a voice so quiet

David had to strain to hear her over the music on the gym's P.A. system.

"I was ready," Jennifer said sadly. "There was nothing wrong with him. There was nothing wrong with us."

David couldn't help but notice how sad Jennifer looked. "What's wrong?" he asked, putting his hands in the air. "We really don't have to talk about this anymore. I was just asking a question about trips. I really didn't mean for us to get—"

"And I've always had this thing," Jennifer said. "I've never dated anybody who was G.U."

"Huh?" David asked, unfamiliar with the term.

"Geographically Undesirable," Jennifer explained. "I've never dated anybody who was unavailable in any significant way. I read that in a book on dating when I was twenty-two."

"Why should that surprise me?" David asked, grinning.

"It's not funny!" Jennifer exclaimed, and then she rolled her eyes. "Okay, maybe it is. But I read that book and it said never date anybody who was in the middle of a relationship, or was just coming out of a relationship, or was married, or was part of a religion you didn't feel comfortable with, or didn't live in your community."

"That limits your opportunities to, what, about eleven guys?" David asked, teasing her.

"Pretty much," Jennifer admitted. "Anyway, you're about as G.U. as it gets."

"I'm also about as mobile as it gets," David said. "I could do my work from just about anywhere."

Jennifer looked surprised. By now, she wasn't pedaling at all.

"Don't you have to be in Hollywood? To get deals? Or whatever it is that you do?"

David shrugged. "I could write from just about anywhere," he said. He thought of his epiphany after talking to his producer. "Maybe I'm tired of the whole Hollywood thing anyway."

Jennifer did not want to allow herself to feel hopeful. "So you're saying…you might not be G.U. after all?"

"I'm just glad you took so long to think through that last proposal," David said, "that you and I are even having this conversation. What if we left it at that for right now?"

Jennifer nodded. "Sounds wise," she said. "It works well with my cautious side."

"If you have any side other than cautious," David said, teasing her, "I still haven't seen it."

Jennifer gave him a dirty look, and then she glanced at the dashboard of her stationary bike.

"Oh, my God!" she said. "My bike thinks I quit!"

"You didn't quit," David said. "You surrendered."

"Well, whatever," Jennifer said, pedaling furiously now. "If we're going to get in a workout, let's get in a workout."

"Fine by me," David said, and he picked up his own pace as well.

"I'm kind of sad," Jennifer admitted, breathing harder now. "You're the first nice guy who has come along. And now you're out of here tomorrow."

"If I ever meet the homeless guy who brought us together," David quipped, struggling to keep up and then dropping back to his own slower pace, "I'm going to thank him."

"I think I saw online that his arraignment is to-morrow morning," Jennifer said. "If you can delay your flight, you might be able to catch it down at the courthouse."

"If I delay my flight, it's not going to be for him," David replied, squeezing her hand. "Can't, though. Story meeting at the studio. Your ears'll be buzzing, because we'll be talking about you."

"Weird," Jennifer said, pondering the idea. "I've gone from being a human being to a story at a studio."

"It could be worse," David said, teasing her. "It could be a Flipper remake."

Jennifer shot him a glance.

After the workout, David drove Jennifer back to her home.

"I kind of wanted to surprise you with something," David said. "I'll come back later. How's seven?"

"Seven's fine, I guess," she replied, mystified. "Do I get a hint?"

"No, you don't," David said, giving her a reassuring grin. "But I think you'll get a kick out of it."

"Whatever you say," Jennifer said, and she gave him a light kiss on the lips and disappeared inside.

Chapter 13

David drove off and returned at six o'clock to his hotel room, where his things were neatly packed for his return home the next morning. He showered and changed into a new outfit, a suit and tie, that he had just purchased that morning for the concert. Sitting on a chair opposite the bed was a bouquet of two dozen long-stemmed roses. With nothing else to do, he put on ESPN and waited for the time to pass.

It was the first time that he could remember having a period of unstructured time. David, for all his seeming nonchalance about time, actually kept to a strict writing schedule, something many writers do. He thought again about his conversation with

Tom—if you could call a one-sided yelling fest a conversation—and realized that maybe he should have used some of his free time to fax preliminary notes on the story. And no wonder Tom was worried: David usually generated at least five pages of notes after the first interview. It's amazing how different things look when you can let go of all the emotional baggage, David thought.

Then he realized why he hadn't taken his usual tack and jotted down a ton of notes right away. He'd been so busy living the story, he hadn't even thought about writing it down!

David chuckled. He was pretty sure that was the first time in his life he'd ever thought those words.

At ten minutes to seven, he went downstairs and stepped into a limo he had arranged for the evening. He appeared on Jennifer's doorstep a few minutes after seven, roses in hand, in plenty of time for the concert.

Jennifer's eyes went wide when she saw how elegantly he was dressed.

"I didn't know you had it in you," she said, teasing him.

"Neither did I," David admitted. "I haven't worn a tie since I was thirteen years old."

"You ought to wear one more often," Jennifer said admiringly. "You clean up real nice."

For a moment, David was silent, admiring the vision Jennifer cut in her floor-length blue dress, silver stilettos, and the sleek up-do she had pinned her long hair into.

"Oh," David said, suddenly remembering himself. "These are for you," and he took the roses from behind his back.

Jennifer was taken aback by the size of the bouquet.

"Are there two dozen in here?" she asked, quickly losing count. "I don't think I've ever seen two dozen roses."

"If there aren't two dozen, I want my money back," David said.

"Very funny," Jennifer said. "Let me put these in water. Come on in for a minute, and then we'll go."

David followed her inside. Jennifer put the roses into a vase she first had to dust off because it had been so long since she had fresh-cut flowers in her home.

"I read in one of those women's magazines," she said, as she trimmed the stems of the roses, "that it's okay for women to buy themselves flowers just to make their homes more appealing. But I'm a traditional girl.

If I get flowers, I want them to come from a man."

"Not just any man," David said.

"Not just any man," Jennifer agreed. She finished with the flowers and turned and handed David a small package—actually, several pages of a computer print-out tied with a blue bow.

"For you," she said. "I didn't really have time to shop, and I don't even know what you like, but I thought you might like this."

"What's this?" David murmured. "What do we have here?"

Jennifer said nothing. She waited for him to un-wrap the bow.

"Directions?" he asked, confused. He unfolded the pages and saw that it contained a set of di-rections from his home in Hollywood to hers in Greenfield.

"In case you ever have the desire to come back this way," Jennifer said coyly. "I figured the directions couldn't hurt."

"Thank you," David replied, taking them and folding them into the inner pocket of his suit coat. "Thank you. That's a very thoughtful gift. The sym-phony awaits."

He took her arm and led her out of the townhome, to the waiting limousine. As soon as the driver saw David and Jennifer emerge, he quickly stepped out from his seat and opened the passenger door for the two of them.

Jennifer, slack-jawed, stared at David.

"A limo?" she asked, amazed. "I didn't even know they had limos in Greenfield!"

"They don't," David said, suddenly nervous that the idea had backfired. Maybe she had a thing against limos. After all, he wasn't in Hollywood anymore.

"I actually had to call around to some nearby towns," he continued. "I hope you like it."

"I've never been in a limo in my life," Jennifer said. "This is really…cool."

David, relieved, gestured for Jennifer to step into the passenger section. It was a stretch limo with all the trimmings—full bar, TV, all the works.

"I feel like I'm going to the Oscars," Jennifer said.

"Some other time," David replied, tumbling into the limo after her. "Let's just start with the symphony for now."

Jennifer sat in the middle of the back seat, looking around, finding the toggle for the sunroof and opening it. "This is so much fun. I wish my kids could see me."

"I could take a picture," David said, and he took out his cell phone and took a picture of Jennifer waving down, her head out the window of the sunroof.

The driver waited for Jennifer to stick her head back inside and safely reseat herself. He drove them to the concert hall, a fifteen-minute drive.

"You really shouldn't have," Jennifer said, her tone one of mocking reproach.

"You've got to live a little," David said. "I just thought it would be fun."

"You've got that right," Jennifer said. "This is awesome. I must sound like such a hick to you."

"You sound perfect to me," David said, and he gave her hand a squeeze.

Suddenly Jennifer looked embarrassed. "I have to admit," she began, "I know absolutely nothing at all about orchestral music. I'm totally tone deaf. I can't carry a tune for the life of me."

"I'm pretty sure you could do a mean job of 'Old MacDonald Had a Farm," David teased. "Or the Barney song."

"Please," Jennifer said, her face a mask of mock horror. "Please don't mention the B word while I'm off-duty."

"Duly noted," David said, grinning. "My mom made me take piano when I was a little kid, and I hated it, but I'm like everybody else whose mothers made them take lessons. I'm really grateful. She gave me a real gift."

"So what exactly are we going to hear?" Jennifer asked, looking out through the heavily tinted glass at her town.

"It just happens to be two of my favorite pieces," David said. "I told you. Beethoven's 7th and Mozart's 40th Symphonies, the G Minor."

"The G what?" Jennifer asked.

"The G Minor," David said. "In the summer of 1791, Mozart had a premonition that he was dying. In that stretch of time, he wrote three symphonies, his Requiem, and a bunch of other stuff—it may be the greatest outpouring of musical genius in the history of mankind. When you hear the 40th, there's almost a modesty about it, which must have been a real change from someone who was a prodigy and a raving egotist for most of his life."

"How do you know so much about Mozart?" Jennifer asked admiringly.

"Just something I like," David said. "Maybe we're not all as shallow as people think, we Hollywood types."

"You never struck me as a Hollywood type," Jennifer said. "You're not my image of a TV writer."

David grinned again. "TV writers are the nerdiest people in the world," he said. "They're just guys who hang out in their second bedrooms and type."

"That doesn't sound nerdy to me," Jennifer said. "Especially if your words are going to be on the big screen. And besides, what's wrong with nerds? I'm a nerd."

"Some nerd," David said, carefully stroking her hair so as not to muss it up.

"What's the other piece?" Jennifer asked. "Beethoven?"

David nodded. "My favorite composer," he said. "Beethoven wasn't deaf by the time he wrote his 7th Symphony—his seventh out of nine—but he must have been experiencing some sort of hearing loss. But that's really to the side. What matters is that it's just incredibly beautiful music. I just can't hear the piece enough."

Jennifer thought about his words for a moment.

"You've heard this piece before, but you want to go hear it again?" she asked. "Don't you get tired of it?"

David shook his head.

"I've got it on my iPod, and sometimes I put it on when I go running on Santa Monica Beach. But I've heard it in concert, I don't know, twenty times. It's my absolute favorite piece of music."

"Isn't it kind of a cliché to like Beethoven so much?" Jennifer teased him. "Do you have a small bust of Beethoven on your computer, like Schroeder had one on his little piano in Peanuts' cartoons?"

David gave her a wry glance.

"Not exactly," he said, now somewhat embarrassed by his show of affection for the musical greats. "I'll tell you what I love so much about Beethoven, and Mozart, and so many of the other great composers."

He stopped for a moment, unsure quite how to put into words his deep feelings for the music.

"Actually, everything about them amazes me," he began. "First, they actually had to hear the music in their heads. They had to hear how the whole symphony would sound, before they could write it down on paper. And they didn't have computers to help them notate

it—they had to write down every note that every instrument played, by hand. Forty-five minutes' worth
of notes for the first violin, second violin, viola, cello,
and on and on, every instrument in the orchestra.

"On top of that, they had to know how to play every instrument, what notes were possible, what would
have been too much of a stretch for the average—or
even a great—violinist or flautist or oboist or whatever. And then they had to have a sense of harmony,
about how to get every note to harmonize perfectly
with every other note. And they had to have musical
ideas, a theme that they would express not with words
but with music, and that way they'd be able to touch
everyone in the world with their music. If you don't
understand English, you can't understand the movie I
write. And if you don't live in this time period, you're
not going to get half the references to the culture or to
technology or to whatever is going on."

Jennifer was listening, rapt, and David did not
even notice that they had reached the concert hall.

"And that's just the work of the composer, hearing
the music in his head and writing it down. Then, when
you think about the orchestra, you've got, say, fifty or
sixty people, or even more, depending on the piece, who

have devoted their whole lives, from the time they were four or five years old, to perfecting their ability to play a musical instrument. The competition for orchestral jobs is so intense that when you go to hear a concert, you're watching and hearing the best of the best of the best. It's like going to a basketball or football game and every player on every team you ever see is a total all-star, which never happens. But an orchestra, that's how it always happens. There are pretty much no weak links in a really great orchestra.

"And then you've got the instruments themselves— all the work and time that the instrument maker put into perfecting his ability to create beautiful instruments that sound so amazing. And then there's the architecture of the hall itself. How you get a space big enough for two or three thousand people to sit, with the acoustics so perfect that anybody can listen and experience a perfect blending of all the instruments.

"And the conductor—who has pretty much memorized every piece of music in a typical repertoire of a typical orchestra, and knows exactly his feelings about each piece, and is able to command the attention of all these orchestra players, who are all individuals and pretty much all of them think they could conduct better than he can. You put it all together, and it's pretty spectacular."

At that moment, the driver opened the passenger door.

"We're here," David said, startled. "I didn't realize I had been talking so long."

Jennifer shook her head. "It was fascinating," she said softly. "I've never heard anybody explain classical music so well to me before. It doesn't mean I'm not going to sleep through both pieces," she said, teasing him. "But at least I know what I'll be sleeping through."

"Reflecting on what has happened up until now, how about just allowing the music to surround you and flow through you and see what happens?" David said, as they stepped out of the limo and headed for the concert hall.

"You've got a deal," Jennifer said.

Chapter 14

Their seats were a perfect fifteen rows from the stage, on the aisle, just far away enough, David quietly explained, to allow the sound to blend perfectly. By the time they sat down, Jennifer had already forgotten whether it was Mozart or Beethoven who had composed the piece they would hear in the last summer of his life. It didn't matter to her, though. She realized she had grown up her entire life and never been to an orchestra concert. And though she had been living in Greenfield all this time, she had never attended a performance of any kind at this concert hall.

The hall itself was beautiful—it glittered like the inside of a jewel box, all blond wood, silver, and red carpeting. It was also vast, seating, according to the program that she quickly skimmed, over 1500 people. Who were these people, Jennifer wondered, as the audience, elegantly dressed, just like the two of them, filed in. What do they do for a living? How do they know about the concert? There must have been something online about it, but if you spend your whole time lurking in dating sites, you don't learn that much about what else is going on.

"I need to get out more often," Jennifer said.

David sat quietly, a look of expectancy on his face as he glanced at the program. Jennifer marveled at him. When she thought of Hollywood, she thought of... well, Hollywood. People who were super cool, going everywhere in limousines, all dressed up. Well, that's what they were, at least for tonight. So that was obviously a part of David's DNA. But there was so much more to him. He loved to laugh—he really looked as though he had forgotten everything in his whole life when he was at the comedy club, just roaring with laughter as Ron Kenney talked about putting his nuts on the belt. On the other hand, she realized, she had experienced that same sense of release while listening to the comedians. The trauma with the gunman, the unanswered question about where her life was heading, what it meant to be twenty-nine and forever single, financial issues—everything that she normally thought about endlessly, especially those lesson plans for her kids—it had all just fallen out of her brain.

The same way it had when she was "in the moment" with the homeless guy in the classroom.

Or when she had meditated in her car, noticing her breath and feeling as if she were "in the flow."

Or when she and David focused on the coolness of the air going into their bodies and the warmth of the air going out.

None of the incidents were isolated. It had started when she kept her cool with the homeless man, yes, but that was only the beginning of a much larger discovery. It wasn't about noticing the air temperature or the act of breathing—those were merely methods or techniques. It wasn't just about David, either...though it was certainly exciting to be with him, because he was smart and fun and incredibly thoughtful, and never tried to take advantage or push the situation in any way.

Jennifer decided that two kinds of magic had descended into her life. First, the release from loneliness, through David's company. But like Cinderella at the stroke of midnight, he was about to disappear back to his way of life in California. She sighed. At least for a moment, she wasn't the lonely schoolmarm, as she sometimes thought of herself in private moments.

But the second kind of magic was something equally valuable, if not more so—a complete release from thought. She realized that she had spent the last who knows how many years of her life just thinking too much. And the more she thought, the less room she made for good things, and good people, to come into her life.

Her life wasn't the problem. Thinking too much about her life was the problem.

Thinking too much about anything was the problem. She didn't think her way into a solution, she realized, with the homeless guy. She didn't think her way into this brief encounter with David. It seemed so counterintuitive, almost anti-intellectual, but the truth was evident: the less she over-thought situations and the more she allowed things to happen, the happier she was. And without David appearing magically in her life, she would never have made that discovery.

Jennifer shook her head in disbelief at everything that had happened over the last two days. What she and David were experiencing together truly made her head spin. His presence in her life hadn't just brought excitement. It had also brought a sense of clarity that was entirely new to her. In the two days since the man had wandered into her classroom with a gun, David had helped her explore the silent and powerful force that had guided her through what might have been a terrifying experience. As a result, she was beginning to sense something within herself that she'd never been aware of before: a kind of ability to be and be present. Bit by bit, what she was realizing was that that silent and powerful force was a part of her. The result was intoxicating.

As they waited for the concert to begin, Jennifer scanned the faces of the other concertgoers, the residents of a world she knew absolutely nothing about. She could learn, she decided. She could learn all about Beethoven and Mozart and know as much about them as all the people in the room, if she felt like it.

And then she caught herself returning to the land of thought and obsession. How easy it was to return to it. Why am I so defensive? She asked herself. Everybody's got their strengths. Not everybody could teach kindergarten, she realized with a smile.

Most people would go screaming from the classroom after just one day!

David glanced at her. "What are you thinking about?" he asked. "By the way, you look so beautiful."

"Thank you," she said. "You look great, yourself. Actually, I was thinking about…thinking."

David grinned his trademark grin. "You were thinking about thinking?" he repeated playfully.

Jennifer gave him a rueful smile. "I think I think too much," she said.

"I could have told you that the first time we met," David said.

"Well, then, why didn't you?" Jennifer asked, rolling up her program and tapping him on the knee with it.

"Because you looked too lost in thought," David said. "You could never have heard me."

"Point taken," she said, nodding. "I probably was. On the other hand, I was going through a pretty stressful experience."

"Most definitely," David said. "Although, I guess I might as well go for full disclosure: Sometimes I think too much, too."

Jennifer raised her eyebrows in mock surprise. "You? No. I don't believe it."

"Well, it's in a different way than you. I'm not so organized. I mean, I don't make lists. I don't organize my spices alphabetically." He nudged her playfully in the arm. "But I obsess in other ways. I make image banks, and think and think about certain phrases that I like. I'm a story-teller, so I love telling stories…but sometimes even I can get carried away. I invent whole histories for people, sometimes. And, to tell you the truth…" He leaned over in his chair. "I'm an artist, you know? So sometimes we let our emotions get the better of us."

"Really," Jennifer said coyly. "You don't say."

"I do say," David responded. "But you've had a pretty positive impact on me, too. Today I was able to let all that go, and just…be in the moment. I wasn't thinking about anything. I wasn't writing any scripts in my head, or imaging what a character would say, or what would be better, a close up or an extra close up. I finally stopped image banking." Jennifer gave him a blank look. "What I mean is, I wasn't thinking about all the stuff I normally think about. I just…enjoyed a calm, thought-free mind."

Jennifer was intrigued. "Really? And that's not something you normally do?"

"Never." David shook his head rigorously.

"And?" Jennifer wanted to know. "How was it?"

"Incredible. It was like my mind became a clean slate. And I just felt so…happy. Like I was at peace with everything. Like I'd tapped into some intense flowing force."

Jennifer nodded emphatically. "Yes! That's exactly it. I've felt the exact same way several times over the last two days. I think it's you," she blurted out, before she could stop herself. She blushed at being so forward.

David took her hand in his. "And I think it's you," he said solemnly. "After I had that moment today, I got a phone call with my producer that would have ruined my day. But somehow, it was okay. I moved past it. I recovered my sense of calm. And I was even grateful for that call. I could see the good in it…which is something I never would have been able to do before meeting you."

Jennifer smiled from ear to ear. "That makes me so happy." Then a look of panic came across her face. "Wait! Is something the matter with the movie you're doing on me?"

David couldn't help but laugh. "Not to worry.

You—and your movie—are perfect." He kissed her lightly on the nose. "And you're not supposed to think so much, remember?"

Jennifer grinned sheepishly. "Oh yeah. How easily I forget."

"So. Are you making a commitment to think less?"

"And allow more?" Jennifer replied. "Most definitely." She paused. "And you? Are you making a commitment to…what is it…'image bank' less and allow more?"

David met her eyes. "Yes," he said quietly. "Yes, I believe I am."

By now, most of the orchestra had ambled out onto the stage, had taken their seats, and were warming up. Jennifer was struck by the seeming contrast between the formality of their attire—they were all in evening wear—and the casual manner in which they approached their task of getting ready to perform the world's greatest music.

"They don't seem to be taking it very seriously," Jennifer said, a touch of reproach in her tone.

"The musicians?" David asked.

Jennifer nodded.

"Oh, they take it very seriously," David said. "You'll

see. They're probably just not thinking about how seriously they take it."

Jennifer gave him a sidelong glance.

"I get the point already," she said. "What are they doing?"

"Just getting ready. There's the conductor."

The conductor, a woman only slightly older than Jennifer, emerged from the wings. She strode to the center of the stage amid a rush of recognition and applause from the audience. She shook hands with the violinist seated to the immediate left of her podium, turned to the audience and bowed, and then turned back to the orchestra and gave them a nod of hello.

"She's so young," Jennifer murmured. "And she's a she. I expected an old man with white hair."

David grinned again. "Life is just full of surprises, isn't it?" he said.

The house lights went out, and after a few moments, the conductor launched the orchestra to the first movement of Beethoven's 7th Symphony. The music had the same effect on Jennifer as had the comedy and the attention she had paid to her breathing while they were meditating—it immediately transported her to a place of non-thought, of simply being present to what

David had termed the greatness of the human spirit. Instead of thinking about the music, she felt it—she felt it in every cell of her body.

She had never heard Beethoven before, at least to her knowledge, and the intensity and complexity of the music had the effect of silencing the internal, endless chatter in her brain, the constant judgments, the constant additions to a never-ending to-do list, everything. Suddenly she understood why David had paid to hear the same piece of music played twenty different times. She could hear it forever, and it would never have been enough. Jennifer had been afraid that the concert would have bored her to pieces. While she might not have wanted to go to the symphony every single night, she understood what David, and what the other 1500 people sitting around them, and most likely what the musicians and the conductor themselves got from it—an absolute freedom from thought, from care, from questioning, from doubt, from fear.

Beethoven's moment on Earth might have ended almost two hundred years earlier, but the music that he had bequeathed mankind brought the inhabitants of an entire concert hall into the present moment, the only moment that really existed. Jennifer blinked rapidly, as if she were a traveler glimpsing a new and unexpected shore. There was not a single thought in her mind.

Except one.

She loved David.

And he was going to leave.

Chapter 15

If the Beethoven had been something vast, like an ocean liner cutting through vast realms of thought, the Mozart, to Jennifer's ear, was something far more sprightly and light-moving, a hovercraft that barely skimmed the surface of the water. There was a lightness, even a playfulness to the music, until she realized that this was one of the pieces David had mentioned earlier, a piece that Mozart had composed within weeks of, and almost certainly with knowledge of, his impending death at an early age. Jennifer could detect the complexity of the music without ever having studied it, but at the same time, there was an underlying lightness, the work of a man who had spent his whole life trying to capture something, translate it into sound, and put that sound on paper.

She was taken by surprise when the concert ended. She had been so transported by the music that the brief moment of suspended silence at the end of the piece felt like waking from a dream. Then the audience burst into wild applause, leaping to their feet in a wave that started at the front of the hall. The conductor took a graceful, humble bow, almost as if to thank the audience for entrusting her with the music. As the orchestra members took their bow, Jennifer wondered what exactly it was that she was sensing in Mozart's music. And then the answer came to her. In the symphony that they had just heard, Mozart's 40th and the second to last before he died, the composer...was allowing. He was allowing the music to flow from some unknown place through his soul, through his intellect, through his fingers, and now through the instruments and into the souls of the audience. Jennifer didn't think these things; she felt them, she knew them.

She turned to David. "That was amazing," she said simply.

David studied her.

"You weren't bored?" he asked.

She shook her head. "I wasn't bored," she replied, as they made their way to the exit. "I was…transported. If that doesn't sound too corny."

David grinned. "It doesn't sound corny at all," David said. "That's what music does. Where exactly did it transport you?"

"It took me out of the thinking that I'm always doing," she said. "It's amazing that I need a whole orchestra just to get my mind quiet."

"You don't always need an orchestra," David said, as they passed through the lobby on the way to their rented limo. "Any good piece of music will do it. A good joke will do it. Even just noticing your breath."

"Hmm," Jennifer said, marveling at how in tune her thoughts were with David's. "You're exactly right."

There was a moment of silence between them.

"I can't believe you're leaving tomorrow," Jennifer said, as they reached the limo, where the driver, standing at attention, had already opened the passenger door for them.

"Let's not talk about that now," David said. "I was wondering if you might care for some post-concert warm apple pie."

A calorie meter clicked on in Jennifer's mind like

a Geiger counter, but she silenced the thought with a smile.

"I'd love to," she replied.

They sat in warm silence on the short drive from the concert hall to the pie shop where they had been before, holding hands and free of thought; just being. Jennifer was surprised by the amount of traffic coming away from the concert hall—Greenfield never had traffic. That was one of the many aspects of living there that made it so pleasant.

For the first time in her life, Jennifer found herself lost not in thought but in non-thought. Yes, David was leaving tomorrow, and yes, there were 560 calories, or 720 calories, or some other number, in a slice of apple pie, and you could add a few hundred more calories with the ice cream and slice of cheese. Jennifer was present with all of these facts yet remained mentally silent – not resisting, not evaluating, just being.

Jennifer was still experiencing the warm glow of the music, and she did not want to surrender the peaceful, meditative feeling that had come to her from the first downbeat of the first movement of the Beethoven.

They were easily the most elegantly dressed couple in the pie shop. As Jennifer lifted the edge of her dress and slid carefully into a small, wrought-iron chair, the few jeans-clad diners remaining in the shop at that hour stared sidelong at her, clearly taken by her lovely appearance. Jennifer barely noticed them. It was after ten o'clock, and normally she would have had a few thoughts about being out that late on yet another school night, but not even those thoughts could penetrate her peaceful state. The waitress, a bright-eyed teenage girl with auburn hair pulled into a tight ponytail, arrived to take their order. She looked approvingly at the two of them, as if they were coming back from prom, even though they were too old for prom and prom itself was still a month or two away.

David ordered two slices of pie and black coffee. When he turned back to her, Jennifer gazed into his eyes for a long moment.

"This has been the craziest few days of my life," she said. "It's been just— I don't even have the words."

"You don't need the words," David said. "And I could say the same thing. I came here for a story, and I got a lot more than I bargained for."

"I'm so sorry you have to go tomorrow," Jennifer admitted. "Is it okay to say that?"

David nodded and gave a small sigh.

"I could say the exact same thing," he replied. "In fact, I will say the exact same thing. I'm really sorry I have to go tomorrow."

"You really have to go?" Jennifer asked in a small voice. And suddenly she felt very sad.

David gave a small nod. "Story meeting at the studio," he said. "They're going to want to know what I've got, and unfortunately, it's not the kind of thing I can do over the phone. For two million bucks, they want to look me in the eye and see what I've got. Make sure I've got something."

Jennifer swallowed hard and nodded. "I understand," she said soberly. "You have a job to do."

For a moment, a feeling of overwhelming sadness threatened to overtake her. She felt it constrict around her throat, her eyes grow hot and sticky, and the horrible ache of loneliness settle into the pit of her stomach. An army of hard and difficult questions plagued her consciousness. How am I going to go back to the way things were once he leaves? She thought. How am I going to function?

But as her mind began flooding once more with thoughts, Jennifer quietly began to ponder a bold new question. "Whose feelings are these?" she asked herself. "Who is it really who's doing all this thinking?"

"Me," came the obvious answer. "These are my feelings."

But then she began to think about what that meant, "mine." What did it mean to "be" Jennifer Albright? Incredibly, her mind, always so ready with an answer, didn't provide one. Instead she found herself more and more present, and to her surprise, her thoughts were actually lessening.

She looked across the table at David. "What is really here right now?" she asked herself. Instantaneously, her mind let loose with a stream of observations of things around her—David looking dapper in his suit, the waitress cutting two gigantic slices of pie in the kitchen, the antique plates hanging on the wall.

But the more she pondered the question of "What is actually here now?", the less she found herself focusing on any one thing in particular. The loneliness and fear she'd felt moments before gave way to a great sense of peace and well-being. Instead of being Jennifer and being terrified that the man she loved was about to leave, she was able to simply be.

She smiled at David. Inside, she was filled with awe and a sense of gratefulness. The situation hadn't changed: she was engaged in a conversation with someone she cared for. But the way she was experiencing it had been completely transformed. Whereas moments before she felt frightened and alone, consumed by her thoughts and emotions, she now felt abundantly peaceful and calm.

To top it all off, Jennifer had the strange sense that she was discovering more and more who she actually was, which actually had nothing to do with her actions or what she was doing or thinking in the moment. It was a crazy idea: that "Jennifer engaged in non-thought" was actually a truer self than "Jennifer engaged in being an over-analytical worrywart"—the second being the Jennifer who had kept a tight grip on her life ever since she started categorizing her paper dolls at age four. She felt like laughing out loud at the very notion—that non-thought was more "her" than thought. If someone had told her a week ago that she'd be saying such a thing, she never would have believed it!

As Jennifer fought—and won—this inner battle, David was watching intently. He felt he could almost sense what was going on inside her head, the intensity and complexities of non-thought waging war on her propensity to over-think things. He saw the struggle, and the release, and the sense of inner joy and peace that spread over her face at the end. And in that moment, he felt it, too.

He reached across the table and grasped her hand.

At exactly the same moment, the waitress brought the apple pie to the table. She was just about to set David's piece of pie down in front of him when he reached his hand across the table to squeeze Jennifer's hand. Eager to avoid setting a hot plate down on a customer's arm, the waitress thought quickly and pulled the plate sharply away. But as she did, she jerked a little too hard, and before any of them knew what was happening, the piece of pie had taken a flying leap off the plate and landed smack dab on the top of David's head. The pie slid to the side and promptly fell off onto the booth. But remarkably, the scoop of vanilla ice cream stayed perfectly in the center of his head, like a tiny white cap in the midst of his thick brown hair.

It happened instantaneously. Jennifer took one look at David, and David took one look at Jennifer looking at him, and in an instant, they both burst into laughter. They laughed so hard that, by the time the mortified waitress came back to the table with a stack of towels, they both had tears streaming down their faces. The absurdity of a ball of vanilla ice cream resting gently on the top of David's head as it slowly started to melt down his ears...it was just too much for them to handle.

In that moment, as they sat across from each other howling and weeping in laughter, they experienced something they had never experienced in any of their former romantic interactions. It was different than anything Jennifer had ever read in a romance novel; different than any real life story in a magazine; and different from all her experiences with past boyfriends. And for David, it was like no script he'd ever written or movie he'd ever seen—he couldn't relate it to anything he had ever felt. There was a sense of absolute oneness and serenity. There were no thoughts. Simply laughter, and happiness, and unadulterated bliss.

Once they got the ice cream cleaned up off David's head, they sat in total silence for a while, beaming. They didn't care in the slightest if everyone at Ellen's Pie Shop thought they were crazy. They'd just shared one of the most amazing experiences of their lives. It was amazing. They both had the same afterglow, and they wanted to hold onto that feeling of peace and joy for forever.

And for the first time, they both realized that it just might be possible to keep returning to that same wonderful feeling, over and over, again and again.

Chapter 16

"You know something, Jennifer?" David said, as they strolled arm in arm back to her home. They'd had the limo let them out a few blocks back so they could take a leisurely walk, enjoying the cool spring night and the bright silver moon.

"Tell me," she said, her head resting lightly on his shoulder.

"Well, I called the airline today," he said with a barely perceptible grin, "and I made the most interesting discovery."

"What's that?" Jennifer asked, not quite knowing where he was going with that remark.

"They'll still have planes connecting from L.A. to

Greenfield the next day. And the day after that. So I…could come back."

Jennifer's eyes widened. In her mind, this evening really was like Cinderella going to the ball, although in this case, it was the symphony, and then she'd be back in her real world again, the limo turned back into a pumpkin, and so on.

"If you'd like me to," David said.

"But don't you have to write your screenplay?" she asked. "I mean, if they paid me $2 million, then they've got to be paying you something as well."

David nodded. "It's nothing like $2 million, I can assure you that," he said, giving her a smile. "But I can do my work anywhere. There's no magic about my second bedroom. I've written entire movies in coffee shops. That's how a lot of TV writers and screenwriters like to work. Otherwise, it would get too lonely."

"It would be pretty lonely if you weren't here," Jennifer admitted. "I'd hate to have to go back to lurking on dating sites."

"Maybe now you'd have the courage to actually say something," David said.

"I'd have the courage," Jennifer admitted, "but

not the desire. Why would I want to talk to any other man?"

She passed a hand shyly over her face. "Oops! I hope that wasn't too…aggressive."

David shook his head. He took her hands in his. "I was hoping you'd say something like that," he said. "I'd really like to come back. The beauty of my work is I can do it just about anywhere. I do have to go back once in a while for meetings, but I could…you know. Rent a place. Actually, I could probably get the studio to pay for it. I'd be soaking up local color."

"You might be soaking up more than that," Jennifer said, giving him a wicked grin.

"I'm not sure I understand precisely what you're referring to," David said, grinning back. "But I certainly like the spirit of the remark."

"Good," Jennifer said. "You really do have a good job."

David nodded. "For now," he said, reflecting on the call he got from Tom. "I don't know how much longer I'm cut out for this whole screenwriting thing anyway," he said.

Jennifer looked startled. "What do you mean?" she asked.

David shrugged. "I don't know," he said. "Just the few days I've spent out here. It's such a peaceful place. These feelings I've been experiencing... they're like nothing I've ever experienced before. The mix of Greenfield and you...it's like a very potent drug. I want more!" He gave her a playful squeeze on the arm and she snickered. "Anyway. I'm sure there's something I could do here in town that would be just as satisfying, perhaps even more so than screenwriting. But maybe I'm thinking too many steps down the checkerboard."

"This isn't Hollywood," Jennifer said. "It's nice, but it's a small town. We don't have any of the kind of excitement that you're used to."

"I don't know about that," David said, staring absently up at the moon. "I spent my whole life chasing excitement, but I'm happiest when I'm experiencing... I don't know what you'd call it. Peacefulness. And anything that brings peace, well, you don't need to be in Hollywood to find it."

"We've got a concert hall," Jennifer said. "Maybe our orchestra is not as good as the one in L.A., but it seemed pretty good to me. So does music. And we get some great rock groups and everything else, if you like that. I don't even know if you do like that."

"I do," David said. "Rock on."

"And there's the comedy club, and, well, there's plenty of air, so you can do all the breathing you want." Suddenly she paused and laughed, realizing what a great salesman's pitch she was making for Greenfield. "Say! What is there in Hollywood that's so special?"

David shook his head. "Aside from the opportunity to meet you, by coming here, I really wouldn't know how to answer that question."

They walked in silence, contemplating the future they were creating.

"If you hadn't come," Jennifer said, holding his arm a little tighter, "right now, I'd be showered and ready for bed, maybe a little lurking on a dating site, maybe going over my lesson plan. And instead, here I am, out with you—"

"Past your bedtime," David laughed.

"Past my bedtime," Jennifer agreed, smiling. "But I'll tell you what I've learned. All that thinking that I did? I mean, it's good to have goals, because otherwise I would never have become a teacher. And it's good to have lesson plans, because otherwise I wouldn't have anything special for my kids to do. So it's not like just drifting through life is a good thing. Right?"

"Right," David agreed.

"I just have to think less and allow more."

"Allow this," David said, and he stopped under a lamplight and planted a passionate kiss on Jennifer's lips.

It was a long embrace, one that attracted a sidelong glance from an older man out for an evening stroll. "Get a room," muttered the cantankerous, solitary fellow. Jennifer and David reluctantly separated, met each other's eyes, and couldn't help but burst into secret laughter, like two chastened schoolchildren.

"Allow me to ask," Jennifer said when their giggling fit had subsided. "Did you really say you're considering coming here for a while?"

"I understand that Mr. Martland quit teaching seventh grade English after he got his 250K, and his position is opening up. I might just apply for it."

"Seventh grade English probably pays a lot less than screenwriting," Jennifer said.

He gave her his teasing smile once again. "Money isn't everything," he said. "Unless maybe you need a little more time to think it through."

"I think I've thought enough for a long time," Jennifer admitted.

"I could say the same thing about myself," David

said. "I learned as much from you over the last couple of days as you say you've learned from me."

"If you say so," Jennifer said.

They had made it to the front of the townhome. Stalling for time, not yet wanting to say goodbye, Jennifer gazed absently around the lawn. She had picked up the litter the reporters and paparazzi had left her with only a few days earlier, but the grass was still trampled and patchy.

"When do you think you'll be back?" she asked quietly, touching the lapels of his new suit.

"Couple of days," David replied quietly. "Maybe three."

Jennifer nodded. "Would you like to come in?" she asked tentatively.

David shook his head. "When I come back?" he asked quietly.

She looked gratefully into his eyes and nodded. "That would be perfect," she whispered, and they kissed again.

"It feels like a Hollywood ending," David said, after the embrace, wrapping his arms around Jennifer.

"Feels more to me," Jennifer replied, glancing up at him, "like a Hollywood beginning."

"I'll have to think about that," David said.

"Don't think too long," Jennifer said, giving him another kiss. "And don't be away too long, either. Once you get back to Hollywood, you'll forget all about me."

David shook his head. "I don't think that's going to happen," he said flatly.

"I was hoping you'd say that," Jennifer said.

"I'll call you as soon as I land," David promised.

Suddenly, Jennifer burst into a wide, ironic smile. "You don't have my phone number!" Jennifer exclaimed. "Would you like it?"

"That would be nice," David said, grinning sheepishly. "That's a first—you spend three days with somebody, and then you ask for their phone number."

"Don't think twice about it," Jennifer said, reaching into her purse, grabbing a pen and a scrap of paper. She scribbled her phone number on it and handed it to him.

"Safe trip," she said.

"You sure you don't need more time to think this over?" David said. "I don't want to put any pressure on you."

"I don't need to think about it," Jennifer said softly.

"When you know something's right, you don't have to think about it."

David nodded.

"It's late," he said. "You've got school tomorrow. I'll call you."

Jennifer nodded.

"It's like I mentioned earlier," David replied. "If I ever see that homeless guy again, I'm going to thank him."

"You do just that," Jennifer said, kissing him again lightly on the lips, turning, and heading for her front door. "You do just that."

As she waltzed up the stairs to her home, she felt truly limitless for perhaps the first time in her life. In truth she felt just like water—flowing and coursing along in a tremendous current toward something beautiful, deep, and profound.

She opened the door to her apartment and realized, with a sheer sense of wonder, that her mind was brilliantly devoid of thought.

Triumphantly immersed in not thinking, she walked down the hallway to her bedroom. Then something captured her attention out of the corner of her eye. She turned and was surprised to see her own reflection. With amazement, she peered into her hallway mirror and saw that she was smiling. She'd never seen a smile so clear and bright on her face before. It's incredible, she thought. I didn't even know I was smiling!

Jennifer realized she wasn't even sure what she knew anymore.

Just then, she could have sworn she heard a quiet voice. It was so soft and gentle, it seemed to be coming from within herself. "Could you allow that to be enough?" the voice asked. "Do you think you could allow that to be enough?"

Jennifer gazed deeply into her reflection as a wide grin spread across her face.

"I don't think it," she whispered. "I know it."

Riding a tide of ultimate peace and freedom, she kissed the mirror, twirled once on the tip of her toes, and floated off to bed.

THE END

Author's Note

We think too much. As individuals and as a society, we approach life as if it were some sort of monstrously complex game of chess, and if we don't think ten or twelve moves ahead, we fear our opponent will, and thus we will lose. The purpose of this book is to help create a paradigm shift that moves away from what I call "compulsive thinking"—the condition of thinking too much (and usually thinking about ourselves!), and the whole win—lose mentality it creates.

The world would be a lot better off if people thought less and allowed more. Individuals would be happier, couples would be more in sync, families would be stronger, and the whole world would be a better place. Is this idealistic or utopian thinking on my part? Perhaps, but the only way we'll find out is if we all committed to thinking a little less and allowing a little more.

Compulsive thought is tied deeply to a compulsive need to over-control situations. The problem with trying to control things is that we can squeeze the life out of a situation, a relationship, or an opportunity, without even realizing it. My thought was to write a traditional self-help book related to the concept of toxic thought syndrome, but I had, you could say, second thoughts about that approach. Actually, I wrote that book, but it didn't feel right. It's just too easy to dismiss the ideas in a self-help book—we can say to ourselves, "That doesn't apply to me." Or "I know somebody who really needs this book!" Or "What does that guy know, anyway?"

A story is harder to dismiss, especially a parable in which the message is not so deeply buried beneath the surface that it takes heavy equipment to dig it out.

This story was inspired by a true account I read of a woman who was rescued after her car spun off the road in a blinding snowstorm. When she told her story afterwards, it became apparent that she had narrowly escaped thinking her way into catastrophe—her initial thought had been to stay in the car and wait for help.

Something inside her told her to get out of the car, and she said later that it was a voice from a part of her brain, or her soul, or some part of her that she had never accessed before. It was an idea that had come to her in a flash of what could be called non-thought. Instead of relying on her thinking apparatus to tell her what to do, she relied instead on her intuition.

Ironically, and tragically, a woman whose car had suffered the same fate, spinning out in that snowstorm, perished because she had made the opposite choice of

staying put and waiting for help to arrive. She died
in her vehicle just a few hundred yards from where
the first woman was rescued. The police officers who
arrived on the scene later said that in situations of
distress, people who think rather than act, can literally
worry themselves to death.

That story had a powerful effect on me, and I began to wonder whether it might be possible to tell a
story of an individual confronted with a frightening,
even terrifying situation, who handled the situation
successfully by shifting unconsciously from thought
and logic to an approach based in non-thought or
intuition. What if Jennifer had created an angry confrontation with the homeless man? Many of us might
have chosen that course—in her position, we might
have yelled at the man, "Get out of my classroom!"
And who knows what the calamitous results would
have been under those circumstances.

So that's why the story begins as it does, with a
person—a very lovely, charming, and respectable
person, to be sure—so addicted to thought that she
has blocked off from her life the things that she really
desires—especially love.

Then came the question of how the story could
function as a parable, how it could teach the lesson.
The traditional approach is to have the "wise man
from afar" come and be Jennifer's teacher. But that's

such a cliché. We've seen it too often. I toyed for a while with the idea of having one of the children in the story—specifically the one who went to the bathroom during the confrontation—be her teacher, but that's also a construct we've seen before.

Instead, I thought it would be best if Jennifer essentially became her own teacher, discovering the power of non-thought and learning three ways to access it from a variety of different sources and experiences. So the little boy teaches her a basic meditative truth, that your breath is cooler when it goes in and warmer when it goes out. Simple, obvious, but deeply profound at the same time, because it offers a fascinating, easy accessibility to the basic concept of meditation, which is to be aware of one's breath. The young child starts Jennifer on her path of discovering three ways to access non-thought. But from there, I didn't think anybody would have really wanted to read a story about a kindergarten child who teaches an adult the meaning of life.

Instead, I focused on the fact that everybody loves a love story, and that along with David, Jennifer would learn two other magnificent means of accessing the realm of non-thought, of quieting what the Buddhists call the "monkey mind" that produces an endless stream of chatter about everything under the sun, without any real meaning or purpose behind all that noise. In my experience, the two most powerful ways of accessing that realm of non-thought are laughter and music.

That's why Jennifer and David spend one evening in a comedy club and another in a concert hall. Several decades ago, the great writer and editor Norman Cousins battled chronic, inflammatory arthritis and autoimmune disease with laughter. He watched old Marx Brother's movies until he literally felt no pain. A person doesn't have to be terminally ill, though, to enjoy the psychic benefits of a good laugh, or a beautiful piece of music, for that matter. Breathing, comedy, and music—those are the solutions I've found most effective in "treating" toxic thought syndrome.

And "treat" is the right word, because paying attention to one's breath, laughing, and enjoying beautiful music really is a treat, if we take the conventionally accepted definition of treat as something special that we only give ourselves or others on rare occasions. If physical fitness is something attained by doing the same sorts of things in the gym or on the running track on an ongoing and consistent basis, we can attain emotional fitness by treating ourselves—in both senses of the term, giving ourselves a bonus and taking the best possible care of ourselves—to the benefits of conscious breathing, great comedy, and the world's best music on a regular basis. The problem is that not everybody knows as much about meditation as they might like, or they aren't sure which comedians to choose. Or, like Jennifer, they might not have a background in classical or so-called "serious" music. For that reason, I have assembled on my website, www. TheMindAtPeace.com, selections of guidance from the world's best meditation teachers, performers of comedy, and great music. I encourage you to make your own personal discoveries as have Jennifer and David, because the gift of meditation, conscious breathing, laughter, and great music is something we can—and should— for our own good and a better world, enjoy every day.

In this story, I make the distinction between compulsive thinking and allowing. I define compulsive thinking as that uncomfortable state in which we find ourselves pondering the same idea over and over and over again, usually without any tangible benefit for all our hard work. Allowing, by contrast, means taking a different attitude toward life. Instead of standing like a sentry or gatekeeper at the doorway to our own lives, we open the door and leave it open, curious about what we'll experience, whom we'll meet, and what opportunities will cross our paths. Obviously, not every person, experience, or opportunity that comes our way is appropriate for us. But I've never met anyone whose life was harmed in the least way because he or she began to allow more and engage in toxic thought less.

So I hope you'll allow these three concepts—conscious breathing, laughing, and the appreciation of great music—to infuse your life with a new level of joy, relaxation, patience, and meaning. As someone who has taught and practiced meditation for decades, I can assure you that the path to everything you desire is as delicate as an inhalation, as joyous as a perfectly delivered punch line, and as full of grace as a sublime piano sonata.

Allow more, think less. It's a recipe for happiness that everyone can enjoy. Thank you for allowing me to share these moments with you.

Sincerely,

Jeffrey Zavik

Breinigsville, PA USA
18 February 2010
232731BV00001B/1/P